# THE MEN WARS

# BOOK ONE
# MEN-IPULATION

# MONICA SARLI

### WITH
### DENISE DOMNING

No Regrets the Book, LLC
9393 N. 90th Street, #102-247
Scottsdale, AZ  85258

Cover photo:
Carrie Reiser Photography
carriereiserphotography.com

Cover graphic design:
Amber Anderson, ADK Designs
adkdesigns.biz

ISBN: 0983909105
ISBN-13: 978-0-9839091-0-1

# TABLE OF CONTENTS

# DEDICATION

This entire book is dedicated to Denise Domning. If it weren't for her belief in me, her support, her commitment, her dedication, her non-judgmental attitude, and her incredible writing skills I would not be here today and this book would never have come to fruition. Thank you, thank you, thank you. Love you, love you, love you. (Love and thanks as well to Ed, who also believed in me, supported me and allowed me to steal his wife for these past six years.)

A special thanks to the people who do their magic on me and make me look like a celeb: Carrie Reiser, photography (you rock, girl!); Autumn Houston of Autumn Hair Studio, Scottsdale; Azure Schaffer, Mac Makeup Counter Nordstrom, Scottsdale; Jimmy of Nail Spa. Special thanks to Phil Zizzo of Zizzo Tailoring in Scottsdale for the camouflage bustier.

I can't mention everyone but to all my wonderful, amazing friends who have cried and laughed with me over the years, thanks so much for listening to me and my stories and letting me make you cry and laugh. To all the young men and women who have touched my life and heart: you keep me young and feeling like I am still Forever 25, lol. Special thanks go to Barb and Alan Ketover, who pushed me, encouraged me and kept me healthy along with finding me Denise Domning. Lilli and Dick Moss, my surrogate parents who gave me love and support during my darkest times. Naya Arbiter and Bette Fleishman, two of the most beautiful and toughest women I have ever met. They cleaned me up, kicked my ass, told me I would make it and taught me to speak my truth so that it may, in turn, help others. After them came Dr. Al Silberman, whose humor at times saved me, who listened to me, supported and guided me. You always told me the truth no matter how much it hurt.

To Steve Sarli, my love and the dear, sweet, dysfunctional man in my life for twenty-five years. You provided me an incredible lifestyle, gave me a second chance at life, and loved me. Thanks for sharing the seat with me in our wild roller coaster ride for all those years and giving me this amazing story to tell. And to the Sarli Family, thanks for all your tolerance, patience, love and support through all the drama for those twenty-five years that I was part of your family.

Lastly, to all of you out there who have and still struggle with your demons and addictions. Don't give up. There is light at the end of your tunnel and no matter how hard it is, you have to keep walking toward that light. The outcome of your life is determined by the choices you make on a daily basis and making good choices will lead you to self esteem, peace and happiness. Set your intention, act *as if*, speak your truth, believe in yourself and live it.

Keep it real. Keep it gangster. Peace out.

# MONICA SARLI

Dark, dangerous, dramatic, intense, provocative, twisted, tragic, but humorous best describes my blessed, amazing life. The title says it all.  My life has been my own personal war with men and sex, one I've fought on the streets, with addiction, through the loss of my loved ones.  More things can happen to me in a week than most people experience in a year.  The best part is that I managed to not only live through it all but live to tell you about it.

My intention isn't just to entertain you.  By sharing my story I hope to connect with all of you out there who might be trapped in toxic relationships, addiction, abuse, denial, fear and shame and let you know that there really is light at the end of that long dark tunnel.  Your destiny and happiness is now and will always be determined by the choices you make.  So make them good ones!

Okay, I know some of you are going to wonder if this isn't the script from some award-winning series on ShowTime or HBO.  Trust me, every story is true, the people and places are all real.  Sometimes I can't believe this all happened but it did.  So get ready for an interesting, thought provoking read and a wild, exciting ride that comes straight from my heart and soul.

I promise.  You won't be bored.

And the saga continues. . .

Monica Sarli
Monica@themenwars.com
www.themenwars.com

# PROLOGUE
# JOHNNY APPLESEED

*December 15, 2007*
*Phoenix, Arizona*

"Now," the nice hospital social worker says in her nicest hospital social worker voice, "how, exactly, did that apple get into his rectum?"

Rhetorical question. All the nurses and doctors who have been in here to gawk at my boyfriend know the mechanics of how items that aren't supposed to be inserted into rectums get there.

And why, I might mention.

Suzy Socialworker stares at me. Her eyebrow lifts, the motion filled with accusation. The doctor standing next to her crosses his arms.

Oh, fuck. I can see it coming. For the second time in my life little five-foot-nothing me is about to come face-to-face with a charge of abuse against a man almost twice my size.

I lift my hands in front of me, palms up, in a gesture of innocence. As if that will help.

"Hey, I didn't put anything anywhere," I tell them both.

"Trust me.  If I'd been home when he"—I wave my hand to-ward the curtained area where my boyfriend is getting sicker by the minute what with that big beautiful, undigested Red Delicious fermenting inside him—"came up with this idea, none of us would be standing here now, wondering how to get it out of him.

Okay, here's what you need to know about the man be-hind the curtain.  My own personal Johnny Appleseed about to become Johnny Hard Cider, claims to be an ex-rock star and porn star.  I can't verify the first claim, but I know the second one is true.  I saw that movie.

Whatever.  One thing's for sure, he really enjoys ex-treme porn.

Viewing it.  Mostly.  He does occasionally get ideas.

He also happens to be English, drop-dead gorgeous, a hard worker and a generally wonderful, loving guy.  I mean, he rubs my feet every night.  And, although it's a little hard to believe at the moment, he's also very intelligent.

However, he is a product of the upper crust British Public School system, an environment notorious for sexual abuse of boys, and he claims to be a descendant of Sweeney Todd, the Demon Barber of Fleet Street.  As far as I'm concerned that explains a lot.

"You're saying he did this to himself?" Suzy asks, still looking incredulous.

Her words stop me.  It's four in the morning.  Johnny and I've been here for hours and I'm tired.  For an instant all that fills my exhausted brain is the image of a man insert-ing something as big as a Red Delicious where the sun don't shine.

When I can't think of anything to say, I shrug and offer, "He's pretty strong?"

It sounds lame even to me.  She doesn't respond.  A moment later she and the doctor walk away, but I'm pretty sure I haven't cleared myself in her eyes.

With nothing else to do but wait for yet another doctor

to appear, I spend the next hours trying to figure out how to prove I really was out Christmas shopping when Johnny got ambitious.

Turns out I didn't need to waste any time plotting. Suzy never comes back and none of my boyfriend's doctors or nurses mentions anything more about the hows and wherefores of his present situation.

Just after dawn the apple makes its exit via surgery. None too soon either. The surgeon assures me that my little Johnny could have died if he'd had to wait much longer. Apparently when fermentation happens inside a body it leads directly to death. There's not even a pleasantly buzzed stage along the way.

Who knew combining fruit and sex could be so dangerous?

Welcome to my fuckingly outrageous life. Everyone in the book exists, although I've changed some names to protect the truly innocent. Every story really happened. You're not going to believe it. Don't worry about that. Half the time I don't believe everything I've lived through and all the shit I've experienced.

I mean, I'm just a nice middle class Irish Catholic girl from Kansas City who should have married a nice Irish Catholic boy and raised a dozen little Catholic kids in the same middle class neighborhood that I grew up in.

Instead, I married a trust fund baby, am recovering from an addiction to Heroin and Crack, was best friends forever with one of the FBI's most wanted drug dealers, almost ended up in the witness protection program and hobnobbed with the likes of Barry Goldwater.

Trust me. You won't be bored.

# CHAPTER ONE
# PULP (NON) FICTION

*Two A.M.*
*Good Friday, 1986*
*Kansas City, Missouri*

I'm sitting on one side of the twin bed in Monk Johnson's guest room while Steve Sarli, my husband of ten years, sits across from me. Monk, our drug dealer, and his wife Faye stand at the end of the bed. It's a fucking slumber party.

Well, not quite although Monk is dressed in a white t-shirt and plaid pajama pants while Faye wears a prim white nylon nightgown under a plain cotton robe. One thing's for sure. We'd all be having a lot more fun if Steve hadn't consumed half a bottle of Wild Turkey earlier this evening.

"Give it to me," Steve demands, snapping his fingers until I hand him the nylon stocking I always carry in my purse for a tourniquet. His words echo in the room. "And don't forget to put the rest of our Dope in your purse."

Steve's voice is always loud, but he's even louder when he's drunk. Noise level isn't the only thing that gets worse when Steve mood alters with alcohol; drink also makes him violent. Tonight while on our way over here, he again threatened to push me out of the car, his father's new Lincoln Continental which we borrowed for the night. At least this time he only threatened. A few years back he actually attempted shoving me out of a moving car, but, thankfully for me, failed at it.

"Hush Steve," Faye warns. She's a pretty woman, small and plump. Her face and straightened hair are the color of tea. When she holds her finger to her lips to indicate quiet she almost looks like a librarian despite her big, fuzzy slippers. "There're kids next door."

"Yeah man, be cool," Monk seconds as he pads over the bare wooden floor to the room's only dresser. It's an oak highboy. This is Monk's business bedroom, where he plays host to his many clients as it were. This room, with its clean blue walls, dark wooden floor, and blue and green patterned blanket on the bed, is one of the nicest places Steve and I have fixed. Big Bill's was the worst with that one room filthy, bloodstained, roach infested shooting gallery. The toilet was always crusted with vomit. You know you have some really good Heroin when you're puking your guts out after fixing. At the time Bill was the only black dealer who'd let us white people mingle with his usual clients.

Monk puts our money into one drawer and begins measuring out our buy from his stash. As always, his movements are relaxed and unhurried. His laid back demeanor is an illusion. He not only looks like the character Samuel Jackson played in Pulp Fiction—he even wears his hair in Jheri curls, those tight little ringlets—he is the character Samuel Jackson played in Quentin Tarantino's movie, albeit shorter and scrawnier. Monk's killed a few people in his time, but only people who fucked with him, or so he professes. According to local gossip, he cut the poor slobs he offed into little pieces. I guess it made it easier to dispose of the bodies.

"Hurry up and give me my shit," Steve blusters. As drunk as he is, his words slur until his command sounds more like *Hurrup n gimmy ship*.

His threat delivered, Steve rolls up his shirt's long sleeve and ties the stocking loosely around his arm while I go back to digging in my purse. Fresh Insulin syringes from my local pharmacy (they think Steve has a sugar problem) along with lipstick and hand lotion, are must have items for me. Always be prepared to party, that's my motto.

I tear open the plastic wrapper off a new syringe and hand it to Steve. Swaying unsteadily, he joins Monk, bracing himself on the dresser as he waits, patient now that he's sure his rush is on the way.

Faye leaves for the bathroom and returns with a glass of water that she places near Steve. Her part finished, she comes to again stand beside me at the bed. I smile at her. She smiles back. I like Faye.

At the dresser, Monk hands a bent, blackened spoon to Steve. Steve takes it then extends his hand, waiting for the paper Monk's now holding. Inside that fold of white paper is our gram of Heroin.

Rather than hand it to Steve, Monk takes a backward step, keeping the thing Steve most wants just out of reach. "Listen to me, man," Monk warns, concern creasing his brow. "This is fucking Black Tar," he says, using another name for what most people call Mexican Mud. "I don't want you doing your usual dose." Monk's always been astonished at how big a hit Steve can tolerate.

Snarling, Steve lunges toward him, trying to snag the paper from Monk's fingers only to miss, his empty hand slamming down on the dresser top. "Just lemme have it," he almost shouts.

Monk would kill any other man for being such a fucking idiot. Why he tolerates Steve isn't that Steve's so much bigger than Monk or that we're such great customers—we always pay first and in cash—or even that Steve always insists on sharing our purchases with Monk. Steve's generous that way. No, Monk treats us right because he's terrified of our new BFF (best friends forever) Terry Kelton, the present drug kingpin of the Kansas City ghetto. That's saying something because it takes a lot to scare Monk.

Monk still isn't ready to hand the Dope to Steve. "I mean it, man. You shouldn't do so much. This stuff's been killing people all over town," he insists.

Steve only takes another uncoordinated swipe at Monk, trying to grab the paper. Monk looks at me, his eyebrows raised in question. I just shrug.

Steve Sarli always gets what he wants when he wants it.

With a disapproving noise Monk reluctantly slides the packet down the dresser top to Steve, who slams his cupped palm over it as it reaches him.

Steve's all business now. As Monk watches, Steve opens the packet to carefully empty some Heroin into the spoon. He then uses the syringe I've given him to draw water up from the glass. This he squirts gently into the spoon. Although I can't see it from here I know the Heroin instantly dissolves in the water. Now lifting the spoon to almost eye level, Steve takes his lighter from his pocket and positions it under the bowl, using the flame to cook his Dope.

The trick is to cook it just long enough to remove the impurities, both in the Heroin and those that were already in the dirty spoon. Steve hates getting spoon shakes, the annoying chill that's caused by dirt in the spoon. Spoon shakes can really mess up your high.

I know the instant the liquid in the spoon starts to bubble because that's the instant Steve drops his lighter to the dresser top. Like a nurse in an operating room Monk's ready at Steve's side, holding out a bit of fluff torn from a cotton ball. With the spoon now resting on the top of the dresser, burning yet another mark into what was once fine wood, Steve takes the cotton from Monk and places it into his liquefied Dope, aims the tip of his needle into the cotton, which acts as a filter, as he pulls back the plunger to draw purified Heroin into his syringe.

Usually when he's done there'd be a little something

left in the spoon, whatever the Heroin was cut with, and God only knows what that was. But this isn't your everyday Heroin; it's not cut with much. There's probably something in it though, because pure Heroin will kill you.

Steve then holds up the syringe and bleeds off the air. From the bed I can see that he's measured out his usual dose; the syringe is about half full of black liquid. That's how Black Tar aka Mexican Mud gets its name: the Heroin comes from Mexico and it's the color of mud or tar, depending on your perspective.

Syringe in hand, he returns to the bed, again sitting across from me. Taking one end of the stocking tied around his bared arm in his teeth and the other in his free hand, he tightens his tourniquet then feels along his wrist.

I watch him search along the thick black marks that cover his inner arm, searching for an unscarred spot along that vein, wondering if this will be the time he won't be able to find a place left to use. Steve's always been a shooter. So many needles being stabbed into his skin over such a long time has toughened his veins and left long stretches of his arms covered in dark, bruise-like scars.

He finds one and pushes the needle into his flesh. As a bit of blood seeps back into the syringe he loosens the tourniquet and the black liquid empties into my beloved husband's body.

An instant later, Steve releases a long, slow sigh. Faye and I sigh with him, both of us relieved. We both know nothing else mellows out a drunken Steve like this. I love Heroin for how it makes Steve normal. I don't think it'd be possible for me to live with him without it.

I watch my husband for a few more breaths, hoping the Mud isn't really as strong as Monk suggests. Steve's eyes half close. His shoulders relax. Then he turns to look at me. All the aggression is gone from his face.

Steve's a handsome man in a John Wayne sort of way, a big man, standing almost six feet tall and weighing in at two hundred pounds, with a strong jaw and a long, straight nose. He's blond even though he's half Italian. He grins at me. It's that grin I fell in love with. On Heroin Steve's again the sweet man I married, the charming boy who swept me off my feet when we first met, the man I now love more than life itself.

"Oh man, that is some good shit," he tells me as the syringe drops from his fingers onto the floor. I hear it roll a little.

I smile back at him, relaxing for the first time since Steve and I left his parents' house to go out for the night.

"I love you, baby," he tells me, leaning over to give me a quick kiss.

"I love you, too, babe," I reply, but he's already deep into his high, eyes closed and humming as he sways gently on the bed.

This is our life, Steve's and mine. We've been partying for all of our sixteen years together. I met Steve when I was sixteen and he was seventeen, the day he appeared at a friend's party with a big bag of Seconal. It was love at first sight, and not because of the Seconal. We've been together ever since although we didn't get married until ten years ago, doing the deed at St. Viator's Catholic Church in Las Vegas. I wore a pale blue knee-length dress; Steve had a suit in the same color. The ceremony almost didn't happen because Steve's Uncle Pete had a hot streak going at the tables. Even late it was still a beautiful wedding, not fancy although Steve's family could have given me fancy. All I wanted was Steve.

My parents didn't attend. Mom couldn't. By then she'd stopped venturing out of the house, incapable of even making it to the corner store for cigarettes. As for Dad, he couldn't bear that Steve's family had money, riches Dad coveted and would never have because he drank up every extra penny he ever made and then some.

Now that Steve's high, I'm ready to alter my mood as

well. Coming to my feet, my purse slung over my shoulder, I glance from Faye to Monk. "You guys want a taste of this?"

Making sure everyone has what they need at Steve's and my parties is part of the job Steve gave me to do in our marriage. His job is to supply the money, while I'm responsible for maintaining the relationships with our dealers and for cleaning up after Steve has finished partying. That means I do everything from getting him home in one piece to making whatever excuses are necessary to cover up when his partying becomes excessive.

"Sure, thanks Monica," Monk replies.

As I expect Faye politely shakes her head no. I'm not even sure she uses. Not many of the dealers' wives I know do. "Thanks anyway, but I think I'm going downstairs to sleep on the couch. Night, Monica, Steve," she says to us with a wave and a yawn.

Steve's still humming to himself, so I say "'Night, Faye," for both of us. Then I reach down and collect Steve's used syringe. Like I said, I clean up after Steve.

After that, I join Monk at the dresser, setting the used syringe to one side. As short as I am, it hits me mid-chest, just tall enough for me to get a good look at the top of that dresser. It's ruined, covered with burns and the black shit that comes off the bottom of spoons where they're cooked.

It's also the perfect height to let me snort my Dope off its surface. I am a dignified Dope fiend. I only snort my shit.

That isn't to say I'm unfamiliar with the act of shooting up. I'll do anyone else. I've injected Dope into the feet, hands, neck, fuck, even the tits of junkies. That needle goes any place there's a vein that isn't too abused to take another stab. I've even seen one junkie shoot up into his cock. If that's all that's left to use, then that's what you use.

As Monk measures out his hit and begins the same elaborate ritual Steve has just completed, I find a small suede bag in that spacious purse of mine. I never leave home without this little bag because everything I need to feel alive is inside it: a small square mirror, a razor blade and a gold colored metal straw about three inches long.

Since I'm not Steve I heed Monk's warning and measure out a small dose—two match heads-worth of Heroin—onto my mirror. I then carefully refold the paper and tuck the remains of our buy into my little suede bag. My razor blade tap-tap-taps as I cut the powder to the texture I want, then I carefully clean and replace the blade in the bag.

I'm obsessive when it comes to my things, whether it's my drug paraphernalia or my shoes. Maybe that's because my mother wasn't big on housework or keeping things clean. Whatever. All I know is that I like things neat. You really can eat off my floors.

Monk laughs as he watches me carefully straighten my lines with the tip of my straw. "Girl, you crack me up. You look like a little college girl doing that."

What he means is that I look fresh and young, not like the hardened Heroin user I am.

"So when are you going to start shooting up?" he adds.

He asks because there's apparently a difference in the high between snorting and shooting. Steve says shooting Heroin feels as good as an orgasm. I wouldn't know and I don't care. I'm not big on needles and I don't want tracks marking my skin.

"This is good enough for me," I tell Monk. "Heroin's still my Boy-friend, even if all I do is inhale it."

He laughs at my pun. On the street corners out here you ask for Boy if you want Heroin and Girl if you're looking for Cocaine. But I'm not kidding. I depend on Heroin. Not only does it mellow out my husband's drunk, when I'm high I'm filled with confidence and strength.

No, I'm Superwoman. There's a reason you can eat off my floors. I swear I could fucking paint the house in half a day on one hit of Heroin.

Now that my lines are ready, I lean down and delicately

sniff one into each nostril.

And instantly rock back on my heels. This stuff's so strong it knocks the air out of my lungs. The inside of my nose feels like it's on fire.

Blinking in reaction, I carefully put away my straw and mirror. It isn't until I'm zipping up my purse that it hits me. If two match heads is this strong, what the fuck is happening to Steve?

I whirl to look at my husband. He's gone from sitting to half-lying on the bed. Although his feet are still flat on the floor, his head is braced against the wall at the head of the bed, bringing his chin almost to his chest. His eyes are wide open as he stares out into the room, or seems to be. Then he gives a big, gasping snore and I realize he's trying to breathe through his pinched windpipe.

The sound brings Monk around to look at him. "What the fuck?" he cries.

"Babe, sit up." I grab Steve by the arm and try to pull him upright so he can breathe. He's too heavy. I can't even shift him where he lays on the bed.

"Wake up," I insist, shaking him. Heroin users are famous for nodding off. "You can't sleep here. We've got to go back to your parents' house tonight."

Steve's parents live on the west side of State Line Road, the street that marks the border between Kansas and Missouri, in Mission Hills, Kansas, a few miles and a whole world away from here. We have to go home tonight because we not only told Ralph and Mary Helen Sarli that we'd be coming back to their house, we've got Ralph's car.

There's not so much as a snore from Steve in response.

"Come on, Steve," I urge.

As I lean over him to get a better grip on his shoulders, his eyes roll back in his head. Then his lips turn blue.

"Monk!" I cry.

Monk's breath hisses from him. "The motherfucker's

O.D.ing!" There's a frantic edge to his voice.

I panic. I slap Steve's face, trying to revive him. "Steve, wake up! You can't die and leave me to explain this."

Steve can't O.D. Not here. Not tonight.

When I get no response I hit him again and again with more power in each slap until I'm almost hammering him with the flat of my hand.

Up until this moment the knowledge that we're using again—everything except Crack; I'll never use that shit again—has been on a need-to-know basis and Steve's parents definitely do not need to know. Steve isn't the only one in the family who expects me to clean up his messes. Ralph, Steve's dad, adores his son and counts on me to make sure the rest of the world never sees the true Steve, the screwup, the child who needed to be institutionalized at fourteen, the kid with learning disabilities so severe that he couldn't graduate from high school and the young adult who flunked out of his first year of college and returned home with nearly fatal cases of Gonorrhea and Syphilis.

It'll kill Ralph to learn that for the past few months Steve and I have been making weekly trips to Kansas City from Tempe, Arizona (proud home of Arizona State University) where we now live. We've been coming here because the Heroin available in Phoenix right now is so bad you can barely cop a buzz from it.

Monk grabs my hand to stop me from hitting Steve again. "It's not working," he says, almost squealing in anxiety, then pulls me off the bed. "Get him up, Monica. We gotta walk him."

I'm beyond thinking at this point. I nod and drape one of Steve's arms over my shoulder. Monk takes the other. We grunt as we heave Steve off the bed.

He's dead weight, forgive the pun.

We're both too short to support him. Steve slips between us to lay face down on the floor. His feet land in front of Faye as she appears in the doorway. Her eyes are wide.

"What's happening?"

I crouch down next to my husband and feel for a pulse. His lips are so blue. I don't think he's breathing. I can't believe this is happening to us.

"Call 911!" I shout to Faye. She leaps toward the phone.

"No!" Monk yelps.

Faye freezes, almost mid-stride.

Monk looks over Steve's prone body at me. His face is as gray as possible for a black man. "Monica, he can't fucking die in here," he pleads. "I got too much Dope in the house. Help me get him outside and I promise you Faye will dial 911 right that moment."

"But how?" Tears flow down my face. "We can't even lift him."

"Got no fucking choice." Monk grabs Steve by one foot and points me to the other. "We gotta drag him down the stairs."

I need my husband to live. If accomplishing that requires getting him outside so Faye can call 911, then Steve is going outside any way I can get him there. I grab my husband's other foot.

It's much easier than I expect. We slide Steve across the smooth wooden floor of the landing to the stairs. Once we start down his body slides bonelessly along with us. He's laying face to the floor. His head bangs on every wooden tread: ka-thump, ka-thump, ka-thump.

Faye holds the front door open for us. Monk and I wrestle Steve through the opening. At the very instant all of him is past the threshold, Monk calls, "Now dial 911!" to Faye.

As Faye runs to do as she's told Monk helps me drag Steve over the cold, frost-slick walkway. Moonlight gleams white on the walkway and turns the nearby barren oak trees to skeletons, bony hands stretching up toward the streetlight beneath which Steve parked Ralph's car. Bathed in that harsh light, the Lincoln's silver exterior twinkles like starlight.

Our breath is gentle clouds in front of us as we huff along, dragging Steve to where the walkway tees into the sidewalk.

Still panting, Monk releases Steve's foot and grabs me by the arms. "Fucking promise me you'll call to let me know how he is," he pleads. He really does care what happens to Steve. Everybody loves Steve when he's not drinking.

"I promise," I say, sniffling. Wringing my hands, I turn and watch Monk race back toward his door. He has the middle unit of these six well-kept brick townhomes. Although Troost Avenue, the boundary street for Kansas City's ghetto, is only a few blocks away, this is a nice little complex, the sort of place that people on their way up to middle-middle class might live.

His door slams behind him. I hear his lock click.

And just like that I'm the only white woman for miles as I stand beside my dying husband with a dozen darkened second story windows staring aghast down at me.

Pulp fiction stole this fucking scene right out of my life, and by now you're probably wondering how I got here.

# CHAPTER TWO
# FRIDAY FIGHT NIGHT

*Summer, 1961*
*Brookside Neighborhood*
*Kansas City, Missouri*

It's Friday night, or rather early Saturday morning. My sister Katie and I are still awake. Mom always lets us stay up late on Friday nights. At eight, I'm in love with the freedom of staying up as long as I want. Katie, who's only four, just likes to tag along with me. But then, Mom makes Friday evenings into a party for us. First, we all paint our fingernails and toenails with bright red polish. Then, as Mom sits in the kitchen and enjoys her beers, Katie and I get to watch as much TV as we want.

I'm older and I love *Elvira, Mistress of the Dark*, and her horror movies, so that's what we watch. By the time Elvira's off Katie's usually asleep and I turn on the old movies. My favorites are the *Thin Man* series with William Powell and Myrna Loy. Sometimes I pretend they're my real parents. Not William and Myrna, but Nick and Nora, the characters they play. I'm not clear as to how I lost my way out of the TV, but I'm sure someday Nick and Nora will find me and we'll all be overjoyed when we're reunited.

Tonight neither Katie nor I are sleeping yet although Mom sent us up to bed a while ago. Our shared bedroom is so tiny that I can hear Katie's breathing start to slow as she begins to drift. My bed creaks as I roll onto my side, staring into the dark.

My bed is crammed under the west window and Katie's bed is pushed under the south window. That leaves my head near her feet. The wooden floor between our beds is covered with a looped rug. Our tiny shared desk has an equally tiny chair. My gaze shifts from the crucifix that hangs over Katie's bed to the picture of Mother Mary holding the baby Jesus that's under the wall sconce by the door. From there I scour the walls, searching out the familiar shapes and patches where our floral wallpaper is peeling.

No matter how tired I am I never fall asleep until Dad gets home. I can't. It's my job to make sure the fighting ends. But Dad's really late tonight.

I shift again, this time to stare through the narrow opening between our door and the wall. I can see a piece of the landing at the top of the stairs. I run my hand over my bedspread, feeling the nubby texture of the chenille as I force myself to stay awake.

The downstairs kitchen door slams. I half sit up. Raggedy Ann slips off the bed. I catch Raggedy Andy and Boo-Boo Kitty before they join her on the floor.

At last! He's home.

I know Mom leaves her perch on the living room sofa to stand in the kitchen's inner doorway, because that's what she does this time every Saturday morning.

"You told me you were going to be home three hours ago," she says. Usually, Mom's voice is high and clear, and little girlish, but not when she's been drinking. Too many beers makes her sound mean, like she hates everyone.

Three hours ago Mom called Cassidy's Bar to check on Dad. That's where he is every Friday night, and most Wednesday nights as well. He loves Cassidy's. He says it's the only place in the world where he gets to do what he wants, which is to work behind the bar, something Mr. Cassidy occasionally allows.

Downstairs, I hear our kitchen table scrape across the linoleum floor as Dad stumbles against it. This is another thing I know because it also happens every week.

"You're pathetic, you know," he retorts viciously in his deep voice, but he's so drunk that his words slur. "Don't you have anything better to do than sit around here sucking on your cigarettes and beer, watching the clock?"

"You told me you'd be here by ten thirty," Mom complains, her voice rising. "What were you doing? Flirting with your girlfriend? That's it, isn't it? You stayed late to be with her!"

I cringe, shrinking down into my mattress. I hate when Mom says this to Dad. She makes it sound like she wants him to leave her. And, us.

There's a rustle across the room. It's Katie, pulling the covers over her head. She says this keeps her from hearing their yelling. I know it doesn't work.

"What were you doing? Flirting with your girlfriend?" Dad mimics Mom, his voice snide, but he's quiet enough that I can also hear the creak of the refrigerator door and the pop and sigh of an opening beer can.

"You don't need another beer."

"I work hard all week. I'll do what I want and you better stop complaining."

"Oh, that's a laugh, you working hard," Mom snaps back. "I'm tired of having to call your boss for you every time you're too hung over to go in. Well, I tell you what. You don't think I do anything, so that's what I'll do, nothing. I quit. I'm not doing that job any more. From now on, you can call him yourself."

"Don't you turn your back on me!" Dad shouts and I hear one of the kitchen chairs hit the floor.

They're scuffling. Upstairs in my bed I close my eyes

and picture them the way I've seen them before, Dad grabbing Mom by the arms while Mom pushes him back from her. Across the room Katie is crying quietly. I throw back my covers, ready to race downstairs and do my job.

If I time my interruption just right, Dad will forget about fighting with Mom as I wrap my arms around his legs. He'll put his hand on my head to stroke my hair and say, "How is my Big Sweetsie?" Katie is his Little Sweetsie.

The trick is in the timing. If I'm too quick, they'll just start back up again after I'm sent back to bed. This time, I'm too late.

Before I can get up Mom cries out again in fright. "Don't! No, Bob!"

There's a muffled thud and Mom shrieks again, quieter this time. An instant later I hear her footsteps as she hurries across the living room floor, then runs up the wooden stairs. Her breathing is ragged as she passes our doorway.

Across the hall the door to her room opens. It's really just our enclosed but unfinished upstairs porch. We call it the sleeping porch because Mom keeps her skinny little bed in there. She says she has to sleep there because Dad, who gets their big bed all to himself, snores.

I sag into my mattress. I failed. It happened too fast for me to stop this time.

Katie creeps across the room, kicking a board game aside as she goes. I lift my blankets. She snuggles up next to me. Together, we listen as Dad climbs the stairs.

He goes into his bedroom and slams the door behind him. I breathe in relief. Everything's happening faster than usual tonight. Maybe they're already finished.

On the sleeping porch Mom's bed creaks as she settles onto it. I wait. I won't feel safe until I hear Dad get into his bed.

A moment later his door opens again. I'm instantly tense. Both Katie and I turn our heads, following the sound of him crossing the small landing. We both expect him to go to the bathroom.

Instead, our door whines as it opens. Light from the hallway spills into our room. Dad's silhouette fills the doorway. As always his shoulders are rolled forward which makes his stomach more pouchy than it is.

I gasp. He's naked. I've never once seen Dad without his boxers on. Neither Katie nor I move we're so stunned.

All of a sudden Mom's standing behind him. She looks so small next to him. Dad's almost six foot tall, but Mom's not even five feet.

"Bob, what are you doing? You get away from there. Go to bed," she says in a loud whisper, as if she actually believes we've managed to sleep through their fight.

When he doesn't move, she gives him a push and he staggers a step or two to the side.

Dad whirls, his fists lifted. "Get away from me," he shouts. "I'm just checking on them."

Then he shuffles out of our view and back into his room. Mom follows, whispering, "Put your pajamas on." The door closes behind her.

Our door remains open wide. Neither Katie nor I can look away from the landing. Now, more than ever, I'm waiting to hear Dad's bed groan and the end of this Friday Fight Night.

"What are you doing?" Mom yelps, sounding surprised. "Take off that shirt. Just get into bed. Stop that. Why are you putting your clothes back on?"

The bedroom door opens. Dad appears in the hallway again, but now he's wearing what he had on this morning, a nice pair of pants and a shirt. His shirt is even tucked in and his narrow belt is in place. Only his black hair is out of place, strands falling over his face instead of slicked back the way he usually keeps it.

Mom follows him out of the bedroom. "Where do you think you're going?" she asks, sounding completely astonished.

So are Katie and I. First Dad's naked, now he's dressed like he's going to work. He's never done this before.

Standing within our field of vision we can see Dad look over his shoulder at Mom. "Shut up. I'm done listening to you tell me what to do. I'm leaving and I'm never coming back. You'll be sorry once I'm gone. You're pathetic. You couldn't whip your way out of a wet paper bag."

His words catapult Katie and me out of bed. Terrified, we race into the hallway, our cotton nighties flowing around us as we run. Together, we throw our arms around Dad's legs. We cling with all our might to hold him in place, to hold him in our home.

"Don't leave us, Daddy," I plead.

All of a sudden, I'm crying so hard I'm shaking. I've never been so frightened in my life. Daddy has to stay. I know that without him we won't have any money, because that's what Mommy always says when she's crying. She doesn't know how we'll live if he leaves us.

"Don't go, don't go, don't go," Katie's sobbing.

He resists for a moment, then he drops his hands to our heads just as always happens when we hug him. Daddy strokes our hair until we both stop crying. Then, he turns and stumbles back into his bedroom. We watch, still shivering and gasping, as he falls across the middle of the bed fully dressed.

Mommy's still at one side of the bedroom doorway. The right side of her face is red and puffy where Daddy hit her.

She sees me looking at her face and raises a hand to cover what will be a bruise in the morning.

"Go to bed, you two," she tells us, her voice quiet but shaking a little, too. Her hazel eyes are red-rimmed, like she's about to cry. "Tomorrow will be a better day."

That's what Mommy always says after she and Daddy fight. Katie and I do as we're told. That doesn't mean either of us sleep. We both lay still in our separate beds listening as Mommy goes back in Daddy's bedroom to undress him.

His shoes thud as they hit the floor. When she rolls him onto his back to open his shirt both he and the bed springs mutter. Then he starts to snore.

I can finally relax. It's over. He can't leave us if he's sleeping.

After a little while I hear Dad's door close, but Mommy doesn't go into her own room. Instead, I hear her go downstairs. With our door still open I can hear her strike a match. The scent of cigarette smoke drifts up the stairs and into our room.

I close my eyes, picturing her sitting where she always sits when she smokes, perched at the end of the sofa nearest the table where she keeps her ashtray.

It's only as I start to doze that I recognize the sound she's making. She's crying.

The next morning everything's normal again. Dad comes downstairs wearing his usual Saturday morning smile. He's wearing a short-sleeved shirt and slacks. His hair is neatly combed, although his face looks a little more swollen than usual.

"Good morning, Big Sweetsie," he says to me as I hug his leg. Then, smiling, he tousles Katie's hair. "And Little Sweetsie." He peers into the skillet on the stove. "Pancakes! They look great, don't they, girls?"

There's no mention of the previous night. After breakfast we start out as a family to do our weekly chores, the same chores we do every Saturday. First, there's a stop at the library for books for Katie and me (and eventually my brother John, who is thirteen years younger than me), then we go to the grocery store. After that, it's back to Cassidy's Bar.

Other families in our neighborhood go on vacation to the Ozarks or Florida. Not us. We do our vacationing at Cassidy's.

Where the fuck else?

While Mom and Dad sit at the bar for a beer or two, using alcohol to repair the damage the alcohol has done to their relationship the previous night, we kids play out back in the alley, turning trash into toys. Then it's on to church for confession and five o'clock Mass.

I couldn't be happier. Mom's right. It is a better day.

# CHAPTER THREE
# NOT MR. ROGERS' NEIGHBORHOOD

*Winter, 1963*
*Brookside Neighborhood*
*Kansas City, Missouri*

In 1963 I've never heard of Mr. Rogers' Neighborhood. No one has. I so admire the real Mr. Rogers. He was an amazing gentle man whose only goal was to make the world a safe place for kids. But his show won't make its debut on public television until 1968.

There was a man in our neighborhood who acted as if he were every child's best friend, a pot-bellied car salesman with a florid face and a circle of naked skin showing on the back of his skull. I'll just call him Mr. P for Predator.

Most of the families living in my Brookside neighborhood are solidly middle-middle class and Irish Catholic, and only Irish Catholic. Italian Catholics have their own neighborhood in the North End.

That makes the ex-Mrs. P all the more interesting to me when she buys a house near us. First, she's one of the few non-Irish folks in the neighborhood. She's from Europe and speaks with a thick accent. During World War II she was in a concentration camp. I know because she shows me the

numbers tattooed on her arm and more than once tells me
stories about being beaten and raped by the Nazis. I love
listening to her tales. I love it when she pauses between hor-
rors and sucks on her cigarette, making its end glow bright
red. She exhales and the smoke curls and winds around her
head, touching here and there on her dark blonde beehive.

Second, she's divorced from Mr. P. That really stumps
me. Why would someone as unattractive as Mr. P, who reminds me of W. C. Fields, divorce such an interesting, exotic
woman?

It doesn't occur to me that she might have divorced
him. In my Catholic world women don't divorce men who
support them no matter how bad things get, especially not
a man of consequence. That's what Mr. P is, a man endowed
with the trust of the People. He's an elected official. A Republican, he represents one of Kansas City's districts in the
Missouri State government.

I meet Mr. and Mrs. P through their middle son. . .I'll
call him Mike. We're in the same class at our local Catholic
School, only a few blocks from Cherry Street. Mike and I
don't know each other well until one bitter winter morning
when my sister Katie and I are trudging to school through
knee-deep snow. All of a sudden Mr. P's car, a brand new
luxury model, stops alongside us. Driving a brand new car is
the nice part of Mr. P's job. Mike and his younger sister wave
at us through the steamy back window.

The car door opens. Mr. P smiles. "You girls want a ride
to school?" he asks.

We sure the fuck do! We both hop into the back seat.

Before long and with my parents' approval, Katie and I
are riding to school in the lap of luxury every morning with
Mike and his sister.

I love it. I gloat as I stand at the front window, watching my uniform-wearing classmates slog their way to school
through Kansas City's changeable weather. Meanwhile, lady
of leisure that I am, I take my time preparing for my day.

Then at 7:45 A.M. my sister and I race down the street to Mrs. P's house. She's always gone by the time we arrive. Divorcees with a mortgage must work.

Mr. P's there, dressed as he always is in a dark suit with a white shirt and a set of pens in his shirt pocket. He's usually sitting at the dining room table when we get there, a box of fresh doughnuts or other pastries on the table next to him. I assume part of his job is to bring breakfast to the dealership.

Once Katie and I are inside the front door, Mr. P sends Mike and his sister upstairs to brush their teeth. Katie and I wait patiently, sitting quietly on the lowest step like the good little Catholic girls we are, for our friends to return. Then we all pile into the big car and take off for school. It's almost like having another family.

Then one day Mr. P sends Katie upstairs with his daughter. "Just go keep her company," he tells my sister.

An instant later Mr. P's holding my hands. He draws me up off the step and leads me into the dining room, maneuvering me into the farthest corner back behind the dark wooden table and its chairs, next to the tall mahogany breakfront that displays all of Mrs. P's good crystal and fine china.

I stand stock still, shocked beyond thinking and staring across the room at the dining room window. Mrs. P always keeps her window shades pulled down and her drapes closed in here. He runs gentle fingers along the curve of my cheek. He strokes his hands down the front of my uniform. It's over a moment later and he's retreating, leading me back into the entry way near the base of the stairs.

It all happens so fast that I don't think anything of it. I can't even put a fucking name to what he's just done to me. I mean, I'm ten. He's a grownup, a charming, funny, powerful adult. All I'm sure of is that it doesn't feel right.

The next day he again sends Katie upstairs and it happens again. And again the next day. Before long it's part of my fucking morning routine: get up, get ready for school, eat my Cream of Wheat, kiss Mom goodbye, go to Mike's house and be molested by Mr. P, then off to school.

As time passes he adds kisses, first to my cheek then to my lips.  By the time I'm eleven his hand is slipping under the bib of my very proper gray pinafore to massage the bumps of what will soon become my breasts.  By the time I'm twelve he's pressing my hand to the front of his pants, making me touch him through his clothing.

"Come on, Monica.  I'm your friend.  You trust me," he says to me as if I'm being unreasonable when I try to turn my face away from him or resist in any way.  There's always a gentle note of pleading in his tone.  Maybe he knows if he's belligerent or aggressive he'll shock me into resistance.

For three years he never goes farther than fondling nor do our encounters last for more than a moment or two.  How could they with the other kids likely to pound down the stairs at any time?  Even so, each one of those moments feels like an eternity to me.

I do my best to escape him.  I ask Katie not to go upstairs, but we're obedient little Catholic girls, well-trained by the priests who confess us and the nuns who beat the begeezus out of us as they teach us.  Mr. P's an adult.  If he asks Katie to go upstairs, then Katie goes upstairs.

For a while I call Mike at 7:00 A.M., and beg him to be ready and downstairs when I get there.  I don't know if Mike is habitually late or if Mr. P dominates his son the way he dominates me.

I don't ever consider telling my parents.  If I can't believe what Mr. P's doing to me then how could I ever convince my parents it's really happening?  Mr. P's someone they respect and admire.  I might as well tell them that our priest is screwing me.

Speaking of priests, it doesn't occur to me to confide in my priest or, God forbid, one of the nuns at school.  The very idea leaves me fucking weak at the knees.

If there's one thing a Catholic girl attending a Catholic

school under the tutelage of Catholic nuns knows, it's that there are good girls and bad girls. Good girls go to heaven because they don't let anyone touch their privates. Ever. Even after marriage. Fucking, except to make babies, is fatal to the soul.

As for the bad girls, well, they're the Devil's handmaidens. All it takes for a good girl to become a bad girl is a single wrong thought and off she goes, straight to hell even if no one ever got around to touching her privates.

But salvation is possible, even for bad girls. That is, if you're lucky enough to get your own personal nun-tormentor to beat the possibility of damnation right out of you. I just happen to have one: Sister Mary Geraldine.

Sister hates me although I'm not really certain why. Okay, so maybe she read the note I wrote, on toilet paper no less—never underestimate the skills of a thirteen-year-old girl—in which I make a play on her name, turning Geraldine into Jellybean.

Or it might have been the time when a girlfriend and I chose to play hooky and go shopping the same day a substantial group of the bad eighth grade boys also skipped school. Sister made what for her was a logical connection. The boys were gone. Monica was gone. Ergo, Monica must have gone with the boys.

I have no doubt she whooped for joy. She finally had the proof she needed. Not only am I a bad girl, I'm a whore, which is what she tells my mother when she calls my house to report my absence. When I arrive home from my innocent little escapade I find my mother waiting at the door, ready to help Sister beat the sin out of my soul.

There isn't a fucking chance in either heaven or hell I'll risk Sister Mary Geraldine finding out about Mr. P, not if I want to live.

I even consider refusing to ride to school any more. Unfortunately, by the time I come up with this idea I'm in love with Mike. This isn't at all the way I felt about my fifth grade boyfriend. No, this is something deeper, something absolute and unshakeable. This is True Love.

So, I tolerate what Mr. P does to me. I tolerate him asking me how big my mother's breasts are then informing me that my breasts will eventually be as big as hers. I tolerate him teaching me how to massage my breasts to encourage their growth. He's hoping this will make my breasts stand tall and pointed.

My eighth grade year is the worst. Not only am I still trapped in Mr. P's daily bump and grind—he's slipping his hand up under my skirt, whispering that he wants to lick me down there now—but Mike's starting to look like his dad. Not even Mike's bad boy costume of black leather and slicked back hair helps. Every time Mike tries to kiss me all I can feel is his father's lips on mine.

Fucking ugh.

The end of eighth grade finally rescues me from Mr. P. Ninth grade means a change of schools. I'll be going to St. Theresa's Academy, walking to school with my best friend and neighbor, Patty. I will never again have to accept a ride to school with him again.

The icing on the cake is my upcoming summer vacation. I'm joining another friend on a trip to Oklahoma City where she's visiting her brother, who just happens to be the only openly gay guy I've ever met. Of course he's a hairdresser.

Ever since I got the invitation I've been working my butt off babysitting so I'll have some money in my pocket when I go. By the time Mr. P sends me a message through Katie that he wants to see me before I leave I've only managed to accumulate the meager sum of nine dollars.

At the appointed time I join Mr. P in his ex-wife's dining room. He's dressed in his summer attire, a short-sleeved white shirt and dark pants, his shirt pocket full of pens. I look at him and in my soul I know it's over. He's never going to touch me again. For the first time in three years I feel safe.

"I wanted to give you something before you leave for Oklahoma City," he says, his smile taking a sly twist.

He reaches into his pants pocket and brings out a hand-ful of bills. He holds them out, inviting me to take them. "Here's thirty dollars."

I stare at the bills in his hand. Thirty dollars! It's a fucking fortune. I want that money more than I've ever wanted anything.

Reaching out, I close my hands over the end of the bills. Mr. P doesn't release them. Instead, he leans closer.

"You can only have this," he whispers, "if you promise that when you're sixteen you'll have sex with me."

I frown at him. I won't be sixteen for three more years and three years seems like a fucking eternity to thirteen-year-old me. Nor am I aware that in the state of Missouri the age of consent for a girl is sixteen. Penetration before that all-important birthday means he could go to jail for statutory rape.

We're eye-to-eye. We're both still holding onto the bills.

For an instant I consider what the nuns teach: any promise I make is my sacred word and I must honor it. If I take the money, then Mr. P has the right to hold me to my end of the bargain.

My whole being rejects that idea as disgusting. And inconvenient.

I really, really need this money.

My eyes narrow. I tell myself that he owes me for all the horrible things he's done to me. I add that someone like him doesn't deserve my promise and that breaking my word to him would be nothing less than vengeance for the wrong he's done to me, even if I haven't yet put a name to the wrong he's done.

My hand tightens on the cash. "I promise," I lie sol-emnly.

His smile widens. He releases the bills. I tuck them into

my purse, certain that I'm finished with Mr. P.

I'm wrong.

Four years later I'm coming home late from a date with my steady, Steve Sarli. I already know I'm going to marry Steve and that he and I will live happily ever after in our drug-induced bliss, because we're never happier than when we're high, and we've been high on everything.

Anyway, I walk in the door, expecting to see Dad in the kitchen. It's his new routine. Instead of doing all his drinking at Cassidy's Bar, he's now also hanging out at our kitchen table, displacing Mom from her bar of choice. He drinks his beer from ten at night until two in the morning sitting in a wooden kitchen chair wedged between Mom's tiny prep table and the countertop. The drunker he gets, the more he pities himself for the awful life Mom and us kids force him to live.

Luckily for me, Dad likes it when I listen to him complain, so he never minds my late returns home as long as I spend an hour or so with him. Also luckily for me, he's usually so drunk that he doesn't notice how messed up I am most nights.

There's method to my madness. If I'm properly sympathetic to his complaints he lets me use our family's one car for my teenage outings.

But tonight Dad's not in the kitchen. Surprised and a little relieved, I make my way upstairs to Katie's and my bedroom. The lights are off. I glance across the room and see the mound of Katie's body in her bed.

Creeping to the end of my bed, I find the Topsy's popcorn can. It's not the lamp that sits on it I want, it's the clock radio. Tonight's the night that Clyde Clifford of Beaker Street is on. He's a DJ for an underground radio station out of Little Rock. If I keep the volume really low I know I won't bother Katie. Or if I do wake her, she'll sit and listen with me. Katie's thirteen now and that's old enough to appreciate Clyde Clifford.

The music whispers into the room. I start to undress,

still feeling pleasantly blissed out. It was Primo Hash tonight.

"Monica?" Katie says as she sits up.

I yelp, startled. This makes Katie jump. She clutches her bedspread, the same blue chenille as mine, to the middle of her chest.

"What's up?" I ask her, doing my best to fake being both cool and sober when I'm neither.

"Mr. P was asking about you today," she tells me, pushing her dark hair out of her face as she releases the spread. She leans over and turns on the lamp. The weak bulb shows me the fine outline of her face. Although I resemble our mother, the older Katie gets the more she looks just like Mom. That means she's pretty, with even features and an oval face, and thin, although I think she'll be taller than both Mom and me when she quits growing.

Now, she looks at me, her gaze locked on my face. "Mr. P wants me to tell him where you work. He says you owe him something and he's ready to collect."

Her quiet words are like ice water over my head. I'm instantly ten again, feeling small, helpless and trapped in Mike's dining room. It's all the worse because I now know exactly what Mr. P wants from me. Only a few months ago I finally gave Steve my virginity, something I held precious throughout my high school years despite all the boyfriends and my getting totally trashed on a regular basis. That's how sure I am Steve and I will marry.

Now as I think about the things Steve and I have been doing together, things that I enjoy, then imagine doing them with someone like Mr. P, my stomach turns.

"What does he want, Monica?" Katie asks, sounding as small and trapped as I feel.

My mouth opens to tell her what Mr. P did to me and the promise I made him. Nothing comes out. I haven't told anyone about him. I don't even know how to form the first word.

Something shifts in my sister's face. "I'll tell you if you'll tell me," she almost whispers.

Her words drive through me. Fuck me! How could I have been so blind? Mr. P didn't lose a victim when I went off to St. Theresa's, he just traded me in for a newer model.

Our stories are remarkably similar. Mr. P, in the dining room, with the donuts.

What I couldn't do for myself I do for Katie. I get angry. Then God hands me a way to get even.

I've been working after school for a printing company located in downtown Kansas City. I'm their Jill-of-All-Trades. I answer the phones, run errands, deliver proofs, sort and wrap completed projects, and generally take care of the front desk. I also tolerate my boss copping the occasional feel.

Our company does a lot of work for local politicians, including printing things like trial ballots and informational pamphlets. Not long after Katie's confession, my boss brings me something to wrap. They're election pamphlets.

I open one. Mr. P's name almost leaps out at me from the paperwork. These pamphlets are for the man running against Mr. P. In that instant I know what I have to do.

The candidate appears later in the day. He turns out to be italian, tall, good-looking and urbane with salt and pepper hair. My boss hands him one pamphlet for final examination. I casually pull out another and study it as if I haven't been fucking staring at it all day long.

As the men read I stare at the pamphlet, mustering my courage. In the back room the printing press is churning out another project. The guys who run the press and the graphic artist are chatting about an upcoming football game, their voices raised to be heard above the steady thrum of machinery. The smell of warm ink fills the room.

I can't wait another minute or I'll lose my chance.

"I can't believe he's running again," I say, my heart pounding in my chest. I remind myself that Katie's the one now trapped in that dining room.

The candidate shoots me a sharp look. "What do you mean?" he asks.

"I mean," I say, taking my time to speak carefully and slowly so neither man misses my meaning, "that he's not a nice man. He likes little girls. He does things to them that he shouldn't."

My voice fades and I choke on the last word. I can't believe I'm spilling my fucking guts to a stranger and my boss when I haven't been able to tell my own parents what Mr. P did to me and is still doing to Katie.

I wait, hoping they understand me. They do. I don't know the whys and wherefores of how it happens. All I know is that once Election Day is over Mr. P is no longer a state representative, and he never again holds elected office.

Don't you be mine, you won't be mine, you won't be my neighbor.

# CHAPTER FOUR
# LIVING ON THE EDGE

*October, 1983*
*Kansas City, Missouri*

"So did your Italian guys finally pay you? You gonna bring me my money?"

The cold, dead voice on the other end of the line belongs to Terry Kelton, Kansas City's present drug kingpin, my dealer and, oddly enough, my friend. I'm pretty sure Terry's a psychopath. He kind of has to be to do the things he's got to do in his line of work.

Right now, I'm listening to his steely tones totally convinced that he's figured out I've lied to him. Terry hates liars. Monk and Red, another of Terry's dealers and the man who introduced us to Terry, both warned me to never, ever lie to Terry.

I can't fucking believe I did it. I wouldn't have if I hadn't been so desperate.

My hand holding the receiver begins to shake. Steve and I owe Terry twenty-five hundred dollars for an ounce of Cocaine that we were supposed to sell, but used instead.

What were we thinking? Oh yeah, that's right. We weren't thinking. We're junkies. We use, we don't think.

And if you think that's fucked up, here's the rest of the story. Steve and I haven't just stolen from our dealer, now we're strung out and won't make it through the month if we don't get more Coke to tide us over. Somehow, I have to talk my psychopathic dealer friend into trusting us with another ounce of Cocaine to sell. If we can get that, we'll do what we always do, cut his ounce of Cocaine until it's two ounces, or fifty-six grams. Since each gram sells for a hundred dollars, that's not only enough money to pay back Terry, but it'll give us six grams of Cocaine to see us through, well, at least twenty four hours.

"The money is what Steve and I need to talk to you about," I say, my heart pounding. My stomach rolls sickly as I force the words out of my mouth. "We just need to come over there and see you."

That's it. I've done it. I've staked my life and Steve's on my belief that Terry won't kill me as long as he's looking right at me.

"Then you better come over," Terry says bluntly and hangs up on me.

I stand there, the receiver pressed to my ear, the dial tone buzzing away, lost in terror. My eyes close as I slowly replace the receiver.

There was a time when Steve's stipend from his trust fund was enough to cover all our expenses: mortgage, food, clothing, drugs—you know, all the essentials. Not anymore. These days we burn through our money faster than ever since adding Cocaine to our list of must-haves. Usually, when we come up short for drug money we ask Steve's dad for an advance, but we've already gone to the Bank of Ralph Sarli this month. We can't make another withdrawal this soon.

But what choice do we have? I was with Terry not long ago when one of his dealers appeared. This guy had the same sort of poor work ethic that Steve and I have as far as selling drugs goes. Terry requested that I excuse myself for half an hour. When I returned I found Terry again alone, as cold and calm as ever, and the apartment newly cleaned.

Looking at Terry didn't save that guy; he stayed permanently missing.

When I open my eyes again Steve's standing in front of me in the kitchen. "What'd he say?" my husband demands.

The reason I'm the one who talks with Terry is because of that division of labor we have in our marriage. Like I said, Steve's job is to supply the money while my job is to maintain our relationships with our dealers so we can buy drugs whenever we need or want them.

"That we should come now," I manage, my voice trembling.

Steve goes gray even though this was what he hoped to hear. "Oh shit," he says and whirls to the cabinet where he keeps his Wild Turkey. He grabs the bottle and doesn't even bother with a glass as he slugs back a gulp or two. Meanwhile, I get my purse and the car keys.

Mario, our black Lab, hears the jingle and comes running for the door, wanting a car ride. He's in luck this time. We don't go to the Ghetto without him. He's not only the theft deterrent for our sporty Datsun 240Z—Mario's basically harmless although he'll bark at anyone who gets near his car—but Terry loves Mario. If Terry does kill us, at least Mario won't be left alone to starve until someone figures out we're dead.

Steve and I leave, dressed in our everyday jeans and t-shirts, and Nikes. At least they're clean. As our habit has expanded and heated up with the addition of Cocaine, our standard of dress has cooled down. But not the cleanliness of my home. You can still eat off my floors.

With Mario riding in the back, his nose pressed in joy to the gap in the car window, Steve and I make our way to The Projects, Kansas City's government housing. This isn't where Terry lives. It's just where he keeps his filing cabinet as it were. Terry's a man on a move, never spending more than two nights in any one place for fear of either being killed by a rival or being tracked by the FBI.

We park, giving our car alarm what might be his last pat from us, and make our way past Lo Gant's place on our way up to Terry's apartment. Lo's husband Aaron Gant, a longtime friend of Terry's, is in prison for murder just now and Terry's promised to keep an eye on Lo and the kids while he's away. Lo needs watching since she has trouble staying sober. A while back Terry beat her silly for leaving the kids alone for a few days while she went on a bender. Not being a user, Terry has no compassion for those who do.

Another set of stairs brings Steve and me to Terry's door. The urge to toss my cookies gets worse. I grab Steve's hand. He looks at me, the same terror I feel filling his eyes.

How the fuck did we get here? Oh yeah. See above about junkies.

At last I release Steve's hand and knock on the door. Terry answers it himself. He's just back from the gym, wearing his sweats and a wife-beater t-shirt, looking like a Black Vin Diesel. As always, Terry has a pair of .45s holstered under each arm. I can't help myself. I find myself wondering if he removes his guns when he lifts weights.

"Hi Terry," I say weakly, then add like the coward I am, "Mario's in the car."

Who knows? Maybe Mario's presence will be enough to make Terry reconsider murder.

Without a word, Terry stands back so we can enter, waiting until we're inside before closing the door behind us.

His place of business is a tidy little apartment, with wooden floors and a few windows. In the open eat-in kitchen is a used metal dinette set: a table with four small chairs. That table's never used for food; it's his cutting table. I've seen at least as much as a couple of kilos of Cocaine on it at any one time. Right now, two of the chairs are set on one side of a large wooden coffee table. On the other side of the table is a sofa upholstered in brown fabric shot through with gold thread and trimmed with Terry's full length mink coat draped across its back.

That's Terry's style: thousand dollar suits under either his mink or his cashmere coats. He even wears a fedora. And, apparently except when he's at the gym, a bulletproof vest. He sleeps in that fucking vest.

None of Terry's usual entourage is here. Most of the time he's accompanied by his bodyguard, who's as straight as he is, and a cadre of hookers. These ladies aren't the raggedy streetwalkers I know from my time spent shooting up in Red's basement, before we made the transition to Red's friends and were invited upstairs to play cards with him. Terry's escorts are the kind you see in films, classy women who look like movie stars or models. If they use drugs, it doesn't show.

My heart pounds harder at the thought of Terry politely asking them to leave the apartment for a half hour, just as he'd asked me that time he'd made his dealer go missing.

Steve and I make our way to the two dinette chairs, leaving the sofa to Terry. Although Terry isn't as big as Steve, his presence fills the room as if he were a much larger man. We watch as he rounds the sofa and sits down.

He still hasn't said a word. There's no emotion on his face as he eyes us. A moment later he casually crosses his legs and lifts his arms until they rest along the back of the sofa.

I can't keep my eyes off those guns.

The quiet stretches. Steve's running his hand through his hair, something he does only when he's nervous. I feel like my heart is pounding so hard it's moving the fabric of my t-shirt. Maybe it is.

Terry tilts his head back, looking at us down the length of his nose. He's a good looking Black man, but you hardly notice his looks against the aura of brutal power he wears like a second skin. His mouth curves into a little smile.

"When are you going to pay me my money?" he asks flatly.

He knows. I'm utterly certain he knows we did the Coke and that I lied to him about it. I gag as the content of my stomach actually makes it up into my throat.

Fighting for calm, I lean forward in my chair. "You know how I told you about these Italian guys and how they might have ripped me off?" I ask, my voice thready as I revisit my stupid lie.

First of all, I can't believe I lied about Joe and Frank. I know and like them. I fucking grew up with them from first grade on. Their dad was a semi-gangster of the Italian sort, the kind of guy you might see rolling stolen tires down a street at midnight, then selling them from the back of his work truck the next day. For a while Joe and Frank followed in his footsteps until Joe finally cleaned up his act. Frank, on the other hand, continues to slide downward, going deeper into gangster-ism than his father ever went.

"Well, that isn't exactly what happened. It was us," I blurt out.

All of a sudden this feels as cathartic as my childhood confessions to our priest before Mass. The words tumble from my lips as if they can't wait to get free. "Steve and I did all the Coke. We're sorry. We'll get your money to you somehow. We'll ask Steve's dad for it."

Fuck me, another lie. We can't ask Ralph for it. Then again, if it's a choice between dying here and begging Ralph to once again bail us out, we'll ask.

I'm still spilling my guts. "I know I should have just told you right up front. I'm sorry. I didn't mean to lie to you. That's why I wanted to come down here and just tell you face-to-face what happened."

I again move forward in my chair until I'm sitting on the edge. It won't be long before I'm kneeling in front of Terry. The resemblance to church just keeps growing.

With every ounce of earnestness I own I say, "You have our word that we'll pay you."

Terry gives the barest of nods. He shifts forward and

removes both those guns from their holsters, then lays them on the coffee table between us. They thud dully as they hit the wood. One of them spins a little as he releases it.

No air is left in my lungs. I stare at the guns. We're going to die.

Steve's breathing in little gasps. It's his turn to lean forward and plead. That's us, penitents, begging the god of Cocaine to forgive us our sins against him.

"Just do it," Steve says. "If you're going to kill us, just do it now and get it over with."

I shoot him a terrified glare. What the fuck is he doing, daring Terry to kill us? Damn him, I wish he wouldn't drink. It not only makes him belligerent, it makes him talk too much. Where's the Heroin when I need it? Not here. Terry won't sell Heroin.

Terry eases back into the sofa. His expression is dead cold as always. His gaze never leaves us. "I'm not going to kill you. Why would I kill you? I like you guys. And Mario's my partner."

As he says this, he smiles or rather offers us what passes for a smile with him. One corner of his mouth lifts just a little bit then he absently strokes his clean-shaven chin. Still, the message is clear. He's not killing us today, but if we ever again to lie to him those guns might come off that table.

I start to breathe again. It's a miracle! Not only will we live, but I'm wagering Terry will give us another ounce of Cocaine to sell and we won't have to talk to Ralph.

It's a good thing that Terry doesn't tell me then that Frank has been working for him.


Here's the whole scoop on how Steve and I end up best friends with Milton Terry Kelton and his twin brother, Hilton Jerry Kelton. By the way, no one calls them Milton and Hilton, not unless they have a death wish. Most everyone in Kansas City who knows them calls Terry Big Twin and Jerry

Little Twin.

I met Jerry first and liked him immediately. He had a casual way about him and was naturally funny. He reminded me in both his looks and his sense of humor of Richard Pryor. He's also a Heroin addict like me and Steve. Terry, on the other hand, always looked like what he is: a cold-blooded killer.

Given their career choice, you might think that the twins had a deprived upbringing. Not so. Terry and Jerry were raised in a nice middle class home by two parents who were married to each other for all their lives. And who worked for the U.S. Post Office. When I met the twins their sister had only recently moved to Chicago where she worked with the Chicago School Board.

Maybe Terry and Jerry were simply bad seeds. What-ever it was that charted their courses, they were confirmed hard-core criminals by the time we met just after Terry and Jerry had completed paying their first debt to society and re-turned to Kansas City. In Terry's case, he'd spent half his life, from nineteen to thirty-eight, in Club Fed for bank robbery.

He started serving his sentence in Leavenworth with Nick Civella, Kansas City's own Mafia Don. From the moment Terry met Nick all he wanted was to be White, Italian and Ma-fioso. Ever since that meeting he's done his best to impress Nick with his professionalism. This includes never dealing in Heroin. The Mafia doesn't approve of Heroin. According to Terry, he also does little side jobs for Nick as a hired hit man, something Terry is proficient at. I think most of his victims end up at the bottom of Kansas City's Swope Park Lake.

It's obvious why Steve and I want to keep Terry as our friend; he supplies our drugs and just the mention of his name is enough to keep us safe in the Ghetto no matter where we go. Terry says he likes me because I'm young, cute and street-smart, the sort of girl any gangster wants on his arm. He likes Steve because Steve's White, Italian and rich. Oh, and Steve's godfather is Al Brandmeyer, once Nick

Civella's reluctant partner in the meat packing business, and I do mean reluctant.

A caveat: to the best of my knowledge the Sarlis were never connected to the Mob in any way except through Al Brandmeyer.

Anyway, the way Steve's dad told it to us, the Sarlis and the Brandmeyers were dining out one night when the maitre d' brought Al the phone. The alarm at his meat packing plant had been triggered. As company president it was Al's job to meet the police at the plant, accompany them as they checked for intruders then reset the alarm.

Ralph remembers offering to go to the plant with Al, but Al said no thanks. A good thing! When Al got there he found a couple of Civella's goons instead of the police. They put him into the trunk of his own car and fired a few shots into the trunk. Fortunately, or maybe by design, they missed Al. It seems Al had been making a serious effort to end his partnership with Nick and this was Nick's way of suggesting that such a separation wasn't in Al's future.

Of course, when Steve told Terry this story he did what Steve always does and made himself sound more important and more connected than he ever will be.

The result? Terry, me and Steve, best friends forever.

# CHAPTER FIVE
## DOING TIME

*Spring, 1984*
*Kansas City, Missouri*

"Hello?"

"Hey, baby. It's me." Terry's voice is as flat and cold as ever.

"Terry! Where are you? What happened? Are you all right?" Terry disappeared about a week ago after a traffic stop gone wrong. Both his disappearance and the mess he made are so not like Terry.

"Shit baby, I can't believe I finally lost it," Terry tells me, sounding almost embarrassed. "Did you hear what happened?"

How could I have missed it? The word has been flying all over the Ghetto. A cop stopped Terry for a traffic violation and it went downhill from there. The Ghetto Times didn't mention what I believe, that the cop who stopped Terry was working for the FBI. The Feds have been jumping through hoops trying to destroy Terry. They, and everyone else who uses drugs in Kansas City, know that right now Terry has Kansas City's fire chief, Gilbert Dowdy, distributing both Cocaine and Crack right out of the firehouses, something Terry likes to call having a fire sale.

Terry goes on, telling me his version of the story. "I was out in the new Porsche." His new red Porsche is only one of the cars he owns. "I couldn't help myself. That car just wants to go fast. But I was only doing a few miles over the limit. The pig turns on his lights. So, I pull over and when he comes to my window I hand him my registration and driver's license. He checked my shit then the motherfucker called me a nigger when he told me to get out of the car." There's a new chill in Terry's already steely voice.

"Nobody talks to me like that. I got out of the car and commenced to kick the shit out of him for disrespecting me that way."

In this case kicking the shit out of the cop means nearly beating him to death. I hope the poor schmuck was getting hazard pay from the Feds.

"It wasn't until the motherfucker was lying on the ground bleeding all over my fucking new shoes that I realized what I'd done." Now Terry does sound embarrassed. Losing control is a rare experience for him.

"I knew that was it," he continues. "The Feds have been looking for a way to revoke my parole and I fucking handed it to them. So I got into the car and drove."

"Where are you now?" I wonder if I ought to be asking this question. Actually, I wonder if the FBI is tapping my phone.

"Mexico," Terry replies.

"Mexico?" Of all places for him to go, I never expected Mexico. Terry's never struck me as a short-sleeved shirt and shorts sort of guy.

"What do you think I should do?" he asks me.

I can't believe he's asking my opinion. In the past year I've graduated from Cocaine to a Crack pipe. It's killing me and I know it. Not that I can stop.

We're Speedballing: smoking Crack, then using Heroin, or alcohol when we can't afford the Heroin, to even out our high. It's all I want to do. That's because the high on Crack is always followed by a horrific low that only more Crack can end.

Eating has become optional and bathing, a waste of time. The only thing I don't let slide is feeding and walking Mario. And cleaning my floor. Our money is always gone before the end of the month these days, and my mother-in-law has started taking me to the grocery store so she's sure we buy food and don't spend the money on more Crack.

It's embarrassing, but not embarrassing enough for me to quit, even though the Sarlis are talking about treatment over at Menninger Clinic. We're still fending them off, but I don't know how much longer we can resist. There's nothing worse or more desperate than broke junkies.

But even on Crack I'm not so delusional to think Terry can escape this one.

"Stay where you are," I reply.

There's no need to think about it. We both know what will happen to him if he comes home.

There's a long pause, then Terry says, "Nah, I don't think I like it here. I'm not into beaches and boats. Besides, it's too complicated here."

Standing in my kitchen in dreary cold Kansas City, imagining the warm, balmy breezes of Mexico, I hold the phone away from my ear and stare at it for a second. Complicated? What's not to like about beaches and what could be more complicating than spending the rest of his life in prison?

Then I get it. Mexico doesn't have the Italian Mafia, it has a Mexican one. Not surprisingly, there aren't any openings in the Mexican Mafia for new drug dealing kingpins, because those positions are already filled with guys who actually speak the language.

Terry likes being a big fish in his particular small pond and he's not keen on crawling his way back up the ladder all over again.

I put the phone back to my ear. "Well Terry, if that's

the case then I guess you'll have to come home and accept what's waiting for you."

He sighs in resignation. From the sound of it I guess he'd already decided to come home before he called me. He just wanted to hear a friendly voice before he comes face-to-face with the rest of his incarcerated life.

"Will you visit me in prison?" he asks.

"Yes," I tell him, and I'm not lying when I say it. Just as it's not wise to lie to Terry, it's also not wise to refuse his requests. We've only done it once, when he asked us to store his Rolls, but we really didn't have room for it and Terry understood that.

Just as we expect, the minute Terry steps off that plane in Kansas City the FBI takes him by the arms. *Do Not Pass Go, Do Not Collect Two Hundred Dollars.* They stash him in jail on parole violation, because their drug trafficking case still isn't ready for prosecution.


*September, 1984*
*Amity Therapeutic Community*
*Tucson, Arizona*

We ended up at the Menninger Clinic in Topeka Kansas not once, but twice. We played nice during the few weeks of our first stay, courtesy of the Bank of Ralph Sarli, enjoying the country club atmosphere and the five star dining. The most earth-shattering thing to come out of this first stay was Steve's diagnosis as being severely Dyslexic. In fact, the doctor informed us that people with Dyslexia this bad either commit suicide or become drug addicts.

Well fucking duh. I guess that fits. No wonder he has so much trouble reading and couldn't graduate from high school.

After a few weeks of being clean we made our escape, promising to behave ourselves once we were back in the real world. We lied. We had only one intention after we left

Menninger: to get high again and stay that way as long as possible.

We achieved our goal and then some. The problem with addicts cleaning up is that if, or when in our case, they return to using, the amount of drugs it takes to keep them high escalates in quantum leaps.

A month later we returned to the Menninger Clinic. Our appearance shocked the staff beyond speaking. Then again by that time we'd both completely given up eating in favor of that next Crack pipe.

While we dried out, the fine doctors at Menninger conferred. We had 'em stumped. Crack wasn't something they'd dealt with before, considering the social group from which they drew their patients.

After another month in the clinic, once again enjoying the pleasant grounds, five star restaurant and comfortable Danish modern furniture in our well-appointed rooms, the doctors shocked us by politely asking us to leave. What we needed, they informed us, was at least a year or three in a therapeutic community. . . if, they warn us, we can find one that will take both of us.

It turns out it's really hard to treat couples who use together. In treatment-speak the couple *contracts-up together.* Translation: the two agree, whether verbally or not, to resist all treatment and escape the facility as soon as possible.

That's how I end up here in Tucson, sobbing uncontrollably as I sit in a circle with seven other of Amity's residents, all of them lowlife convicts who, unlike me and Steve, have been stipulated into this program.

For them this place must be like joining the military. For me, I think I've died and gone to hell. It's hot, hard and horrible, and Steve and I have agreed to live here for as long as it takes and that could be years.

Oh, help.

"Monica, what are you feeling?" Bette Fleishman asks

me.

Unlike the rest of us who sit in metal folding chairs, Bette always brings her own rocking chair when she leads these days-long sessions. Dark haired and eyed, dressed in her usual Amity uniform, black crop pants and a gray button-down shirt, she's in her late thirties. Raised in Los Angeles the privileged daughter of a prominent LA attorney, Bette looks like she should be living in one of Tucson's nearby ranchettes. She doesn't look like someone whose mere glance could turn any one of us addicts into a pile of quivering jelly.

I know she can. I've seen her do it. Fuck, she's done it to me.

She gets out of her rocker then makes her way to the outside of our circle and walks slowly behind our backs. I can't help thinking she looks like a black jaguar, lethal and lovely.

She and her partner the beautiful Naya Arbiter are the two toughest bitches in all of Arizona, or, fuck me, maybe the world. They, along with Naya's husband Rod Mullen, run Amity. All three of them are graduates of Charles Dederich's little charm school, Synanon, one of the original drug reha-bilitation programs, which tells you a lot.

Amity, well Naya actually, was the only one willing to take on a married couple. Steve and I are here because Naya loves a challenge. She's sure she can break us.

"Talk to me, Monica," Bette continues, her voice sooth-ing and quiet. "Tell me what you're feeling."

Bette has one resident-turned-intern on her way to be-coming a counselor helping her lead this marathon session. We eight in the folding chairs, their victims for what Amity terms a retreat, have been held captive in this room for more than three days now. Our prison is one of Amity's casitas, basically a one bedroom, one bathroom cabin with a kitchen built against one wall of the great room. The windows, es-pecially the bathroom window, are all too small to crawl out of, not an accident, although that hasn't stopped people from trying.

I can't answer Bette. I'm crying so hard. For the past three sleep- and food-deprived days, fueled only with lots of coffee, we've been working on all the fucking bullshit that happened in our lives to make us addicts. I'm not crying because I'm tired, although I am exhausted. I'm emotionally shot. Every horrifying story, every tale of abuse has started to feel like a dagger being shoved into me. Everyone's pain has become mine.

I swear the walls of this room ooze blood, so much pain has been spilled in here.

Right now I'm torn asunder over my fellow inmate reliving how her drug dealer dad killed one of his people, leaving her to clean up after him. Bette spent the morning forcing her to describe every gory detail. What the brains looked like, how the blood stained her skin, how it smelled and felt. She's had to do it over and over again.

Why? Because these details are what caused her to fall, to return to using, after years of sobriety. For a long time, she'd worked as a counselor in another program.

So I cry because I feel, no, I know that she's as lost and helpless as I am. She's as broken as I am. What happened to her stripped any and all sense of normalcy from her life. She can never get back what her father stole from her, just like I can never get back what my parents and Mr. P took from me.

All of a sudden, Bette's putting a pair of chairs in the center of the room.

Panic tears through me. Fuck me! She can't make me do this. No, I won't do this. I can't.

I shoot a terrified glance at the nearest window. Out! I want out now.

The intern appears at my side, her hand on my arm. I want to shove her away, but I can no more do that than I can get out the window. Still, I resist, forcing her to half lift me from my seat. She has to hold me up as we make our way to that chair in the center of the room.

I'm terrified. My heart, already banging away from a caffeine overdose, starts tripping in earnest.

One of the guys in the room takes the opposite chair. He's a tall, redheaded young man, a stipulated convict. Like all of the convicts Bette and Naya treat, his conviction included a drug crime or a crime committed to support his habit.

Once he sits, we're so close that our knees touch. We have to be. My soon-to-begin torture requires me to be restrained, to prevent lil ol' me from landing any untoward punches.

He grabs me by my forearms. I reluctantly curl my fingers around his arms, feeling his cotton shirt sleeves against my palms. My fear of what's about to happen fuels my tears. I gasp for air. My eyes run. My nose runs. My chin trembles.

Let the psycho-drama begin!

Bette leans down to whisper in my partner's ear. His pale eyes, so different from Mr. P's, are focused on me. "Would you like a ride to school today? Come into the dining room, I have some doughnuts."

"No, I don't want to," I say. My words have dual meaning. I don't want to relive my time with Mr. P any more than I wanted to go to Mrs. P's house every morning all those years ago.

I hate it here. I'm tired of being one of the few White women in this place, of being mocked because I didn't grow up poor or in the Ghetto or on the Rez. Or, being taunted because Steve and I live a different life and I can't do without the Lancôme products Steve's mother faithfully sends me since I've been at Amity.

Seriously, I can't live without those products.

No one at Amity, not Naya, Bette, none of the residents, can forgive me for bringing our own bed linens. It's not that we don't want to use the donated castoffs that everyone else uses, it's just that their resources are so limited and Steve and I have so much.

Pseudo-Mr. P pauses. Bette again whispers in his ear and he cocks his head to listen. "Come on, just touch me here. It'll be our secret. No one will ever know. I'm your friend. You can trust me," he repeats.

"No," I retort. My tears are still flowing, but now they burn. "I can't trust you. You're not my friend."

My hands clench tighter around his arms. I try to lean back. As he pulls me forward one of his knees slides between mine. The contact is electric.

It's like someone put a volcano inside my chest. My stomach rises. My anger explodes. I'm fighting back from him, but he's stronger than me and keeps pulling me forward.

I don't see the young man any more. Instead, the man in the chair in front of me is a pot-bellied car salesman with a florid face and a circle of naked skin showing on the back of his skull.

"No," Mr. P says to me, "I've never been your friend. I used you like I used all the other little girls. I never cared about you just like your father never cared about you."

With each word, my anger spirals. I'm not crying any more. I'm panting in rage.

"I knew your father wouldn't protect you. No one protected you. You're worthless. You were nothing to me. When I was done with you I threw you away, just like I threw away your sister when I was done with her."

I lunge for him. He's so startled he releases my arms. I flail at him, my closed hands landing with bruising impact. He yelps and tries to shove me off him. Instead, he and his chair fall backward onto the floor. I'm on top of him, hitting and kicking with all my might. I dimly hear people shouting. Someone's trying to grab my arms.

"I hate you," I scream, crying at the same time. "You fucking bastard. You robbed me of my innocence. You fucking asshole!"

Bette's got me by the back of my shirt, dragging me away from him across the floor. I'm not done. I send another vicious kick his way and feel my foot connect with his leg. "I'm going to kill you for what you did to me and to my little sister!"

Now that I'm too far from him to reach him my bravado collapses. I curl in on myself, sobbing, my arms crossed over my broken heart and aching stomach. Lying on the floor in the fetal position, I cry like I'm dying, or like my insides are being ripped out of me, which is how I feel.

I hate this place. I hate this pain. I hate having to confront this over and over again, even though a part of me knows this pain is why I use. I can't live with this inside me and I can't make it go away, so I use Heroin, Cocaine or whatever else is at hand to make it tolerable.

Bette murmurs quietly to me as she helps me rise to sitting. Once I'm upright, she puts her hands on my shoulders to brace me in place. I can see through my tears that I'm no longer the only one in the room having a nuclear meltdown. There isn't anyone here who hasn't been seriously damaged by someone who supposedly loved them or someone they trusted. Everyone is crying. A couple of addicts are in the corners, their backs to the rest of us because they can't bear to look at me and what I'm feeling.

The intern has my co-participant sitting upright on the floor with me. Once again he's a young redheaded man, only now he has a fist-sized mark on his face that I suspect will darken to black before the night is over.

Bette's hands tighten on my shoulders. "Monica, what is it you want to hear Mr. P say to you?" Right now, she sounds every inch the matron she appears to be. Her tone is smooth and calm and compassionate.

I hear these things in her voice and I believe. Bette loves me. Bette knows me, she'll protect me. That doesn't mean I'm ready to speak. Although I'm trying to control my tears, all I've accomplished is to give myself hiccups.

"Tell Mr. P what you want to hear from him," she insists. "Look him in the eyes and tell him what you want to hear."

I look at the young man. I'm still terrified, but this time it's different. Bette's here. I'm safe. And what Mr. P did to me will never happen to me again. Never.

"You hurt me. You used me," I start then pause to catch my breath.

Bette whispers in my ear, "Tell him you didn't deserve this, that it wasn't your fault this happened."

"I didn't deserve this," I repeat, then add my own version of what she's saying. "I was just a little girl. It's not my fault that you did this to me."

"Tell him that you trusted him and he betrayed you," Bette prompts.

"I trusted you and you betrayed me. That's something I'll have to live with for the rest of my life."

"Now," Bette whispers, her wonderful voice sending waves of reassurance through me, "ask him to tell you he's sorry and that he'll never again do that to anyone."

Power rushes through me. Does it come from me or the dragon-bitch behind me, the one who doesn't let anyone fuck with her babies? It doesn't matter. For the first time since my tenth year I'm not afraid of Mr. P.

"Tell me that you're sorry and that you'll never do this again," I demand.

My pseudo-Mr. P doesn't wait for the intern to whisper his answer. "I'm sorry," he says, tears in his eyes. "I will never do this again. Please try to find a way to forgive me."

With that he smiles at me. The shadow of my own pain touches his eyes and all I can think is that I want to hug him. I reach out to embrace him and he comes readily into my arms. We hold each other, crying, for a few moments then I apologize for hitting him. He forgives me.

When it's all over, I'm freer than I've been in a long while, but bits of shame over what Mr. P did to me still linger. I can feel them hiding just beneath my stomach. Never again doesn't feel as certain as it did a few moments ago.

But, just for this moment, I've never felt so safe in all my life.


*June, 1985*
*Amity Therapeutic Community*
*Tucson, Arizona*

"Just buy us two plane tickets to Kansas City that we can pick up at the airport, and wire some money to the Western Union office in downtown Tucson. We'll need that to get something to eat at the airport," I say quietly into the phone, stifling my urge to glance furtively from side to side.

It's essential that I look like I'm having an official Amity conversation. In fact, I'm standing at the desk to make sure everyone can see me. At the moment I'm actually across the street from Amity proper, at the Circle Tree Ranch, once the Westinghouse family's winter retreat. Amity is leasing the property. The phone and desk are in what we call the Hub, once a small sitting room when the family resided here. I, along with another resident, have been appointed by Naya to manage this property

"Are you sure that's enough?" The voice on the other end of the phone is Ralph Sarli, my partner in The Great Escape.

"Positive," I reply, my voice filled with the pretense of confidence.

There's no guarantee that we're even going to get out of here, much less have enough money to avoid the minions of Amity who will surely come after us once we've escaped the compound.

I'm not even certain how we're going to make it to the Western Union office. If I can't find a way to get a bit of cash, we'll be stumping our way from this far, wild end of Tucson to downtown.

There's a pause on the other end. Then Ralph begs,

"How is Steve?"

Amity is too far from Kansas City for Ralph. He and Mary Helen came to visit about six months ago. They rented two rooms at a lovely nearby resort, hoping we would join them for the weekend. But we're not getting out of here until Naya and Bette deem us cured. As far as Bette was concerned that second hotel room was proof Steve's parents intended to kidnap us. She stayed at our sides when they came on campus to visit us.

"He's ready to come home," I reply, not really answering Ralph's question.

I can't answer Ralph's question, not when Steve says he's been at Amity for the entire year because I have a drug problem. Fuck me, like he painted those tracks on his arms to look tough?

As for me, I'm as ready to leave as Steve. Last month Steve and I finally regained the right to sleep together. Separating us is how Naya hoped to circumvent the possibility of us contracting up together and failing to enjoy the full benefits of their program. I don't think it worked. Here we are back together again and the first thing we're doing is planning to get out.

It's actually Naya's and Bette's fault that we want to go, or at least that I need to leave. They're pushing me to start counseling others and demanding that Steve and I get ready to move into their halfway house in downtown Tucson.

No fucking way am I living in some seedy place working at some minimum wage job when Steve could be buying us a house in Tempe, one with a pool.

That's it. I want a house with a pool. I'll lay out every day while Steve does whatever Steve wants to do.

"Make sure the tickets have no date," I remind Ralph, "just in case we don't make it out of here on schedule. I've got to go. See you soon."

The day of our departure arrives. When no one's looking I dash into Mark Schettinger's office to shove my hand into his change jar and pull out a handful of coins. I don't count the coins until later. I snagged about thirteen dollars. That's more than enough to get us on the bus.

Get on the bus. The phrase sends a wave of guilt through me. Getting on the bus has special meaning here.

Naya considers Amity her home and in her mind there's no greater sin than for someone to dirty her house, meaning bring drugs onto campus or come onto campus high. When that happens, Amity goes into lockdown mode. Naya keeps us all in one room, the doors bolted then sets out folding chairs arranged to represent the seats on a bus. She surveys us, pointing out the people who have to get on. Translation: prepare to be interrogated and get your head shaved.

Shades of Synanon!

Steve's ridden the bus. I haven't, although I didn't escape interrogation. All it took for me to cave was the threat of a head shaving. Actually, the possibility of losing my waist length hair may have been the real reason I've stayed clean this past year.

No more of that fucking shit. I am so out of here.

I start across campus to the house where Steve and I are sharing a room, and enjoying sex for the first time in our marriage. That could be because it's the first time we've ever had sober sex.

Just my luck, I run into the two young guys who are the night watch this evening. Night watch here includes opening every door and counting bodies. The longer Steve and I have before we're discovered missing, the better our chance of reaching the airport.

"Hey guys," I say to them, flashing them my sweetest smile. "I have a favor to ask you. Steve and I, well, tonight, we're going to be busy." I put special emphasis on the word.

One of the boys blushes. He's young, not yet eighteen, and not nearly as tough as he'd like me to think.

"Would you mind skipping our room on the first

round?"

They're charmed and they both respect me enough to give me the chance I need. I don't even feel guilty any more.

Steve and I know all the routes out of here by now. As soon as darkness falls, we creep out, make our way to the road and trek up to the convenience store close to the nearest bus stop. The hours drag as we hide behind the dumpster, taking turns watching as Amity's fleet of white vans patrol the streets looking for us.

Dawn brings the first bus of the day, and we're on it. A quick stop at Western Union and we have the money Ralph sent, then we're on to the airport. Within three hours we're flying out of Tucson for Kansas City. A crying, grateful Ralph meets us at the airport, and we're back in Oz again.

I wait a week before I call Bette to tell her where to send our things. It was a mistake.

"You'll die, Monica," she says, laying her curse on me. "If you and Steve use again, you'll instantly go back to the level you were using at when you were at your worst and then it will get worse from there. Use, and I guarantee you'll both die."

# CHAPTER SIX
## CLEAN UP

*Two-thirty A.M.*
*Good Friday, 1986*
*Kansas City, Missouri*

Bette's curse has finally caught up with us. I look down at my unconscious husband, lying on the night darkened sidewalk. My breath clouds in front of my mouth. There's no cloud visible above Steve's lips.

I want to kneel down beside him and feel for a pulse. I can't. I'm terrified there won't be anything to feel and I'll have to accept that he's dead. I can't even conceive of life without Steve at my side.

Who would I be if I wasn't Mrs. Steve Sarli?

I may not know who I'd be but I know what I'd be: completely and terrifyingly alone. All that work at Amity and the corner of Mrs. P's dining room still haunts my every breath.

Just then the wailing ambulance careens around the corner and pulls up behind Ralph Sarli's Lincoln. Two EMTs jump out. As one of them opens the back of the ambulance, the other guy rushes over to me, only to stop and stare at me in disbelief.

Like I said, I'm the only White girl for miles.

"Hurry," I urge him, "my husband's dying."

That spurs him into movement. He drops to one knee next to Steve and feels for a pulse. I watch his fingers shift on Steve's neck as he searches.

My knees start knocking. My legs weaken. Fuck! Steve's dead. I just know it.

"What did he take?" the EMT demands, looking up at me.

Lost in terror for Steve and myself, his demand startles me into offering more information than I might have given under other circumstances. "He drank a half of a bottle of Wild Turkey earlier tonight, then did Mexican Mud."

The minute the words leave my lips I get an unwelcome glimpse of the truth I've done my utmost to avoid since running away from Amity less than twenty-two months ago.

There is nothing dignified about a Heroin addiction. A junkie is still a junkie no matter how well she dresses, how big her bank account or how nice a house she owns. Shame floods me.

Instead of disgust the EMT gives me a brusque nod and says, "Thank you very much." His words are clipped and his voice, sincere.

"Get the Narcaine," he shouts to the guy at the back of the ambulance.

I'm so taken aback by his unexpected reaction that I can't stop myself. "What's Narcaine?"

"A wonder drug," he replies, again going down on one knee so he can roll Steve onto his back. "If you get it into 'em soon enough it completely stops an overdose. That is, if someone bothers to tell us what's going on in the first place so we can get it into 'em." He glances up at me. "So, thanks for letting me know."

His co-worker drops off their medical kit then starts back to the ambulance to retrieve the collapsible gurney. My new best friend takes the bottle from the top of the kit—Narcaine, I presume—then gets out a syringe. As he forces his needle in one of Steve's heavily scarred veins, Steve grunts. Relief floods me. I close my eyes as my hands start to shake. My husband still lives!

I fucking love this EMT.

"Where are we taking him?" the other one asks me.

"To St. Luke's," I reply. I know a doctor who works out of that hospital, or rather the doctor knows Steve's sister.

"Will you be riding with us?"

I glance at my father-in-law's Lincoln. I'm already in deep enough shit as it is. I'll really be fucked if the car also disappears, which it's likely to do in this neighborhood.

"I can't leave the car," I reply, then realize I'll be walking if I don't get the keys.

While the EMT checks Steve's IV, I lean down and retrieve Ralph's car keys from Steve's pants pocket. As I come upright I catch the distant wail of sirens. The sound grows steadily louder until a police car turns onto Monk's street. It pulls to a stop behind the ambulance. Two policemen get out.

"What's going on?" one cop asks, watching as the two paramedics wrestle Steve onto that now unfolded gurney.

"Overdose," my EMT buddy replies.

The other cop wanders over to check the license plate on my father-in-law's Lincoln then strolls back to the cruiser. The two of them lean together against the side of their patrol car and stare at me.

My heart pounds as I wait for them to ask me what a little Irish girl from Brookside is doing standing here in front of a known drug dealer's house where White girls shouldn't be, especially in the hours just before dawn and especially not with almost a gram of Heroin in her purse.

Neither cop says a word to me. They just watch as Steve is loaded into the ambulance.

What's wrong with this picture?

One side of the ambulance's double doors closes. The light stays on inside and I can see the mound of Steve's body.

As one paramedic starts toward the driver's side of the truck my new friend closes the back door then joins his partner. The siren starts up and they're off.

There's no reaction from any of the surrounding town-houses. People here don't bother to look. Looking either gets them in trouble or is a depressing reminder of what they already know is happening around them.

I hurry over to the Lincoln. Neither policeman moves to stop me. Thank God. It wouldn't take them long to figure out that I'm in no shape to drive.

I carefully make my way to St. Luke's, park the Lincoln then enter the emergency waiting room where I wait. And wait. And wait.

There's light in the sky before a pair of doctors appears in the doorway from the emergency room's inner sanctum to call my name. I'm on them in a heartbeat.

"I'm Mrs. Sarli. How's my husband?" I demand.

"He's in Intensive Care for the moment. He's stable and he'll live," says the one who called my name.

I'm almost dizzy with relief. It's a fucking miracle, nothing less. Bette's wrong again. Steve and I have managed to dodge death one more time.

If I weren't a junkie I'd be wondering how many more times we're going to be able to manage this, but I am a junkie so all I feel is relief. No need to make changes yet. All I need right now is to touch my husband and confirm for myself that he's alive.

I look up at the doctor. "Can I see him?"

"That won't be possible," says the other one. He stares at me the way I expected the paramedics to look at me, as if I'm pond scum, which, as a seriously addicted junkie, I suppose I am.

"What happened tonight?" the other asks. It's not a question, it's a demand.

Frowning, I glance between them. What the fuck kind of question is that. Like they don't already know what happened? Like they can't tell from the tracks on Steve's arms?

"He overdosed on Mexican Mud," I say, stating the obvious. Hey if that's what they want, that's what they'll get.

"What else?" the first doctor demands.

"Nothing," I retort, starting to get angry. Who the hell are they to tag team me? If the cops didn't have anything to say about Steve's overdose, then why should these fucks?

"Steve and I were out. Steve had a few drinks which he followed with too much Heroin. I want to see him," I say, making my own demand.

They both cross their arms and frown down at me. It's hell being short. I don't need a fucking dictionary to translate their body language. There's no way I'm getting past them.

"How about you tell us who beat him up," the taller one says, staring at me as if he already knows the answer and that answer is. . .me.

Truly shocked, I stare up at them. How could either of them assume someone my size could do any harm to Steve, who is so much bigger?

"I never laid a hand on him," I protest, but the minute the words are out I remember.

I not only slapped Steve silly, I dragged him face-first down the stairs.

Ka-thump, ka-thump, ka-thump.

Fuck. I did batter Steve, just not the way these two pricks think.

"Go home," the shorter one says. "Come back tomorrow." His tone says there's no way in hell I'm getting into see my husband, no matter what I say or do.

I fume as they retreat through the double doors, going where I'm not allowed to be. Who do they think they're fucking with? No one is going to keep me away from my husband.

What I need right now is my own Cleaner.

The two ER doctors are barely out of the waiting room before I rush for the nearest pay phone—remember those?—to call Dr. Joe at home. Never mind that it's obscenely early in the morning. I know he won't mind.

"Hello?" he answers sleepily.

I say, "Joe, it's Monica."

No last name needed. He knows who I am.

Then I add, "Steve's at St. Luke's and the doctors won't let me see him."

"I'll be right there." He doesn't even ask what happened.

Why an up-and-coming doctor like Joe so readily gives up his warm bed without hesitation for me has to do with Steve's family.

Steve is the grandson of Rocco Sarli, and Rocco is one of those Horatio Alger success stories that America is so famous for.

Rocco arrived in Kansas City, the land of meat and potatoes, as just another poor Italian immigrant, taking up residence in the city's north side Italian district. It didn't take Rocco long to figure out he wasn't the only man in his neighborhood hungry for the foods of his homeland. That's when Rocco, along with Thomas Basile, the father of Rocco's future wife Nicolena, Peter Vagnino and a few other Italian pals, founded the Kansas City Macaroni and Importing Company.

By 1917 the company had gained a nationwide reputation for its pasta. In 1920 Rocco's company merged with another pasta firm out of Denver. This new company took the name of the Denver firm: American Beauty. The packaging was emblazoned with a single red rose, a symbol Rocco chose to honor his new daughter Rose.

The company ticked along through the Great Depression but boomed after World War II when all the vets who'd served in Italy and tasted the heaven that is spaghetti returned home wanting pasta on their tables. After Rocco died, his widow Nicolena performed the merger of all mergers: she married Peter Vagnino, one of the firm's partners. Nicolena said she did it to protect Rocco's business for his only son Ralph, Steve's dad. She told me part of the conditions of this marriage/merger was that Ralph would become the company's president and CEO when he came of age. And that's exactly what happened.

By 1969 American Beauty was the sole pasta supplier to the U.S. Military and the company that put the ABCs in Campbell's Alphabet Soup. Then in 1979, Ralph sold his father's company to the Dough Boy.

That's right, Pillsbury. The sale included a fifty million dollar stock exchange.

Thank heavens for Nicolena! Because of her business sense and foresight the Sarlis still held a majority share of American Beauty. That meant that the five Sarlis, Nicolena, Rose, Ralph and his two children—took home fifty-one percent of both the purchase price and the stock exchange. That nice little chunk of change made Steve's family, already more than comfortable, bona fide rich people.

Well, not all of the Sarlis, at least not immediately. Ralph convinced both of his kids to tie up their portions of these new riches in trusts that won't expire until 1991, the year of Steve's and my fifteenth wedding anniversary. Gold diggers need not apply here.

For now, Steve and I live off the interest from the trust which we get as a monthly stipend. That more than covers our bills, leaving plenty for us to stay as high as we want— as long as we avoid Crack—as often as we want, which right now is pretty often. We even have the fluidity to make loans to cash-strapped drug dealers.

Money is indeed a very interesting tool.

About a half an hour later Dr. Joe walks into the hospital waiting room. Even this early in the morning he looks good, tall, dark-haired and very doctor-ish in that confidence-inspiring sort of way. I like him. I really like that his ethics keep him from mentioning to Steve's family how many times he's seen us at the local university Methadone clinic where he volunteers.

Hey, we're not the only Heroin addicts in town who turn to Methadone when Heroin's scarce.

"What's going on, Monica?" Dr. Joe asks as he joins me.

"Steve overdosed," I say, only to once again dog paddle in a sea of shame.

A year. We were clean for a full fucking year and now we're right back where we started, sort of. This is all the fault of Bette's curse. If she hadn't said anything we might have been able to just do Heroin on the weekends, recreationally as it were, the way we planned.

I swallow my regrets. "The doctors won't let me in to see him. They think I beat him up."

Dr. Joe looks startled. "You? No way."

I'm glad someone's certain I'm not the sort of person who would ever beat my husband. Inject him with Heroin, any time. Beat him, never.

"Come on," he says, taking my arm.

Together, we blast through those fucking double doors, going straight into the ICU. As Dr. Joe pages through Steve's chart and listens to the nurse tell him that Steve should be moving out of ICU later today, I slip around the bed to stand at my sleeping husband's side. I stare at Steve, stunned.

My poor precious husband looks like he's gone through a windshield. Both his eyes are blackened. My gaze catches on the tiny cuts that mark the edges of his eyes. At first I can't imagine what caused these until I glance at my hand. I'm wearing a large, square ring made of gold and turquoise. When I hold my hand up to the side of his face the cuts are a perfect match to the edges of the ring.

Blue and yellow coloring dribbles down his face, over his jaw line and down his neck. His hospital gown gapes and I can see bruises on his chest. I again hear the awful ka-thump of his head against tread.

Fuck! No wonder they thought I'd beat him.

Dr. Joe joins me at Steve's bedside. "He's actually doing quite well, considering what happened to him." There's no hint of judgment in his voice when there ought to be.

Like I said, money really is an interesting tool.

My high is just a memory now. Without Heroin to blunt my shame, the thought of breaking the news to Steve's family that we're using again is more than I can face. Telling the truth just isn't on my list of things to do this morning.

I look up at Dr. Joe. "You have to call Ralph and Mary Helen for me and tell them what's happened. I just can't do it, not just now," I add, softening what is for all intents and purposes a command.

Joe responds just as I expect. "Be happy to," he says with a smile.

"Thanks," I reply in truly heartfelt relief. I'm a fucking coward and I know it. "Joe, I'm going to get a room and sleep for a while. I'll be back in a few hours."

"I'll let the nurse know. You won't have any problems when you come back," he assures me.

I retreat to the hospital parking lot and drive Ralph's Lincoln to the hotel across the street where I check in. Once in my room I take care of the one thing that definitely is on my list: I call Monk and let him know that Steve is still alive.

"I'm so glad, Monica," Monk practically coos with delight.

As well he should. A good customer has been saved to use again another day.

With that chore finished, it's time to take another tiny snort of Heroin. I deserve it. It's been a hell of a night.

In a minute I'm buzzing again. I don't even consider going to bed, although I haven't slept in twenty-four hours. Sleeping would end my high and that would be a shame and a waste. Instead, I use the hotel's complementary soaps to clean up and bide my time until nine. I'm going shopping.

Not just anywhere. I'm going shopping at the Plaza.

I love the Plaza. It was built in the early days of the twentieth century by J. C. Nichols, who took one look at his first automobile and understood that cars were not only here to stay, they would change the face of American daily life. With that in mind he designed a complex of stores to accommodate this new mode of transportation.

That's right. J. C. built the first shopping mall. Back then what he designed was an open air shopping mall, which of course was superseded by indoor malls, which go out of fashion to be replaced by. . .open air shopping malls. What goes around comes around.

To me, shopping at the Plaza is like taking a trip to Europe. That's because J.C. modeled his mall after Seville, Spain. Water trickles in tiled fountains. Statuary decorates corners. All the stores' facades are tiled and covered in stucco.

So as soon as the clock chimes nine, I'm strolling along walks that ooze Old World elegance. Store by store, I buy the essentials: toothbrush, hairbrush, undies and such.

I truly, truly am a fucking coward. Everything I just bought I already have. It's in my suitcase at my in-laws' house.

I'm back at the hotel by noon, just in time to get Dr. Joe's call.

"Monica, Steve's been moved to a private room and he's conscious," Joe tells me.

I rush back across the street where I find Steve in his new hospital room. He's sitting up in bed. An IV tube runs into his arm. Underneath his awful bruising he looks haggard and drawn.

I don't mind, because what he looks like to me is alive. I smile at him. "Hey. You look like death warmed over."

"Hey," he replies, smiling back, "I am death warmed over."

We laugh then my laughter dissolves into tears. I collapse to sit on the side of his bed. "I almost lost you," I tell Steve, my head bowed as I stare at my clasped hands. "Then the doctors wouldn't let me see you this morning. They thought I hurt you. When I couldn't get to you I thought I'd die. I don't know what I'd do if you had—" I can't bear to finish the sentence because I hate thinking about Steve dying.

Steve leans his head against my arm. His hand closes over mine. "I promise, babe, we'll never be separated again," he says, doing his best to soothe me. "I love you."

That only makes my eyes leak again. He twines his fingers between mine and I relax against him. We sit quietly, just feeling each other. In that moment I'm more in love with him than I've ever been.

"So tell me, what the fuck did you and Monk do to me?" Steve demands gently. "Look at my face. What did you do to me?"

I press even closer to him, not wanting to see his reaction to what I have to tell him. "First, I tried to revive you by slapping you, but it didn't work. Monk wouldn't call 911 until you were outside, so we had to drag you down the stairs. You went down on your face."

I can feel him flinch against my back. "Shit. I think I'm glad I was out." Then he gives another flinch. "Oh, fuck! What did you do with my dad's car?"

"In the hotel parking garage," I reply, looking at him from over my shoulder.

We stare at each other for a long moment. I can see it in Steve's eyes. He's no more excited than I am about confronting his dad.

Just then his nurse bustles in. She's a chatty, friendly thing. When I mention I'm staying in the hotel across the street, she says not to waste my money. Within minutes she's ordered another hospital bed for Steve's room so I can stay with my husband. What a difference this is from the suspicious doctors earlier this morning and all the more reason to give thanks to Dr. Joe.

Two hospital beds shoved together aren't quite the same size as a queen, but it's not space I crave. I snuggle up to Steve, loving the weight of his arm over my shoulders and basking in his promise that we'll be together forever.

# CHAPTER SEVEN
## LA FAMIGLIA

*Mid-Afternoon*
*Good Friday, 1986*
*Kansas City, Missouri*

Spooned together, watching TV is how Ralph and Mary Helen Sarli find us later that afternoon.

Mary Helen enters and comes to a stop near the door to Steve's bathroom. She's tall, slender and attractive. As always when she's out, she's dressed in her about-town wear. Today it's a spotless, perfectly creased pantsuit, no doubt purchased from Harzfeld, an iconic women's store based in Kansas City. Not a single fair hair is out of place. In every way Mary Helen epitomizes country club casual. As well she should. She and Ralph are members of the Indian Hills Country Club in Mission Hills.

Mary Helen is very much a product of a generation fanatical about keeping family secrets. Although her upper middle class upbringing was touched with tragedy—her father committed suicide when she was young—she'd never consider talking to anyone about the experience, especially a professional listener like a psychologist or psychiatrist. Shed a tear in public? Never! As far as Mary Helen is concerned, emotions are only tolerable when kept under tight lock and key.

The only time she lets up on the reins is when she's drinking, at their country club or at home. Her favorite time of the day is cocktail hour, which at the Sarlis starts precisely at five. At exactly four forty-five, Mary Helen, dressed for the evening in heels and a skirt, descends into her family room. She opens the louvered bar doors and retrieves her ice bucket.

Her heels tick purposefully as she crosses her kitchen floor to the refrigerator. The freezer door creaks as it opens. She retrieves her ice cube trays. With a resounding crack the trays give up their frozen bounty as the cubes clatter into the ice bucket.

Tick, tick, tick, Mary Helen walks back to her bar, places two ice cubes into a fine Waterford Crystal highball glass. Scotch follows, carefully measured in a sterling silver jigger. Her jigger is one of her prized possessions. No tarnish is ever allowed to dim the best part of Mary Helen's day.

If Ralph is home she serves him first. If he hasn't yet arrived, she pours herself her first drink then retreats to the smaller chair in the family room, the one placed where she can look out the bay window at the driveway. Sipping, she sits there, waiting for Ralph.

Once Ralph is home, the liquor flows. And flows. That jigger is hard at work until late in the evening, well after dinner is over.

Drinking takes the edge off what it costs Mary Helen to be Mrs. Ralph Sarli. Mary Helen is a WASP married to an Italian man raised in Old World traditions. Did she know when she married Ralph the sort of expectations he'd have of his wife? There's sex of course, but what about the way Ralph expects her to satisfy his needs before he considers satisfying any of hers? That is, if he even considers her needs. He expects to get everything he wants the moment he asks for it, and she must never question or challenge anything he wants; she's just supposed to deliver.

And, of course, she must put up with his mother.

God knows, that wasn't easy. Nicolena told me before she died that she never liked her daughter-in-law. Like the rest of us in the family couldn't tell? We could all see that nothing Mary Helen did ever pleased Nicolena.

I don't think it was personal. I think it just was a clash of cultures. Mary Helen was too WASPy for an Old Country Italian woman, and Nicolena was too Old Country for Mary Helen to accept. Also, Nicolena told me she faulted Mary Helen for encouraging Ralph to drink too much. Yeah right, like Ralph couldn't find the backbone to say no to his supposedly subservient wife?

Ralph Sarli follows his wife into Steve's hospital room. He's short, balding and stout, his features much softer than Steve's. Steve's the spitting image of Rocco, which made him Nicolena's favorite.

Ralph may be small and portly but he carries himself like the captain of industry he is. He's also dressed as if he's on his way to their club, wearing a blazer over a pressed shirt and creased twill pants. Maybe that's where they're off to after this visit. They eat dinner at their club a few nights a week. Much of the rest of the week they take their evening meals at local restaurants.

Mary Helen is Ralph's bartender, not his chef.

For a moment, Ralph and Mary Helen just stand and stare at us. I wait for the recriminations, the yelling and tears. There's nothing but silence.

At last, Ralph squares his shoulders and steps closer to the bed, a smile fixed on his lips and his eyes filled with resolve. I see it happen. Ralph is a warrior, preparing for battle, ready to do what he must to save his screwup son, which in Ralph's case means mostly writing checks. These he signs with a flourish and his deep, everlasting love for Steve. He's written checks to pay off Steve's numerous DUIs, to replace the cars Steve's wrecked, and to fund our three stabs at rehab.

Ralph loves his role as the patriarch, the captain who rescues his passengers just before the ship runs up against the rocks. He thrives on the crisis and feeds on the drama. That's good, because wherever Steve is there's drama. Ralph really shone the time Steve got busted for selling Cocaine. Ralph jumped right into rescue mode, hiring the best lawyer in Missouri. Oh yeah, Steve is the perfect child for a man who loves to fix really complicated things.

Now, Ralph takes his precious son's hand. His fingers don't flinch away from the thickened and discolored veins that mark his son's inner arm. I watch Steve shrink in front of my eyes. In an instant a helpless and incapable little boy replaces the man who is my husband.

It reminds me of that time Ralph brought out the home movies. Documented on those reels were a few of their frequent trips. That is to say the trips they took as vacations, not the trips they made across the country to check on manufacturing facilities or the posh trips they make to the Pasta Conventions. (Like any other business, there are conventions for pasta makers. They're very cloak and dagger, everyone trying to scout out the newest shape or flavor of the year.)

I watched the images play, my heart breaking for little Stevie and his sister. Each of the trips began with the children weeping and waving as their parents left them yet again. To this day I wonder if Steve thinks of the household's black maid as his real mother, but even she was just part-time. Business and grownups were king in the Sarli household.

"Are you alright?" Ralph asks his son now, speaking gently. "Joe says he'll release you tomorrow."

"I'm fine, Dad," Steve replies, all the life gone from his voice. He sounds like what he knows he is: the kid who could never, will never, live up to his beloved father's expectations, the man who was incapable of following his father into the presidency of American Beauty.

"I guess you are," Ralph replies, his lips trembling a little as he smiles.

"I guess so." Steve gives a childish shrug. He's played this role so often in his life he knows his part by heart.

I glance at Mary Helen. She's still standing where she stopped. As near as I can tell she hasn't moved a muscle. She's watching her husband and son, but her face could be carved of stone. I think if Mary had been given a choice, she would have long since cut Steve and me off until we cleaned up on our own, but Ralph will never allow that.

Ralph gives Steve's hand a squeeze and steps back from the bed. As he turns to look at me his entire manner shifts. He's no longer the doting father, but the competent CEO.

"You two are coming to our house for Easter dinner, aren't you?" His tone makes the family gathering sound more like a trip to the gas chamber than a celebratory meal. As always, he directs his question to me, thereby once again defining my role in their family. I am Ralph's most trusted ally in his battle to save Steve from himself.

Mary Helen shakes off her granite to make a sharp sound of disapproval. "What about his bruises?" she asks. "How are we going to explain his bruises to Aunt Rose?"

Aunt Rose, Ralph's sister, is Italian, childless and a widow. That's three strikes against her as far as her Italian family is concerned. They treat her like a naive child. Never mind that Aunt Rose has been an integral part of American Beauty from her early childhood. When it comes to family problems, i.e. us, Rose supposedly doesn't have a clue.

Right. Like she didn't know it was Steve and me who stole the prescription drugs from her medicine chest each time we visited?

Ralph frowns and looks at me. "What do you think?" he asks me, ignoring Steve who stares sulkily at his blanket-covered feet. Ralph waits for me to do the most important part of my job for him: coming up with plausible excuses or explanations for anything untoward Steve does.

All of a sudden I wonder why the fuck I was so afraid to call Ralph this morning. Ralph wants, no, needs to keep rescuing Steve, because the minute he stops he'll have to confront the fact that he can't save his son. He never could. The only one who can save Steve is Steve, and he's not trying. As for Mary Helen, she simply can't afford to care anymore. It hurts too much. They're as addicted to their denial as Steve and I are to Heroin.

Shaking off my surprise, I step into the job Ralph has made mine. "Tell Aunt Rose that someone ran a red light at the Plaza and hit us, and that Steve went through the windshield."

I glance at Steve and find he's watching me, a small smile lifting his lips. He's remembering the last time we used this excuse. It was after Steve had been pistol-whipped at Big Bill's, a then favorite shooting gallery of ours. The junkie who attacked us was high on Ritalin, of all things, and wanted Steve's expensive watch.

If Ralph remembers having heard this excuse before, it doesn't show. Why would it? Steve's had so many accidents and DUIs that nothing specific can possibly remain.

He nods. "That'll work," he says almost happily. "So, I'll see you both tomorrow at dinner, then."

Before Ralph turns away, I pull his keys out of my purse and offer them to him. Ralph waves them away. "You keep the car. You'll need it to get home tomorrow."

With that, all is forgiven. I give my in-laws hugs and kisses. They both tell me that they love me. And I know they do. Who else would do so much for addicted me except someone who loves me? I tell them that I love them, too, and I mean it. They're as much my family as my own parents.

They're hardly out the door when Steve looks at me, his expression carefully blank. It's a sign of how much Ralph's visit has stressed him out. Putting some distance between us and his father's suffocating love for him is the reason Steve wanted to live in Tempe.

"Have you got that Dope with you?"

I give Steve the eye. What does he think? That I left it in the hotel for the maid to find and steal? "Of course I do. It's in my purse."

"Get it out," he says, already cleaning the spoon from his lunch tray.

I pull out the packet, but hesitate before handing it to him. "Steve, promise me you'll be careful this time. This stuff's so strong."

He grins at me, his eyes practically twinkling as he turns on the charm. That's one thing Steve has in spades. He's a charming and genuinely sweet man. Everyone who meets him loves him for that, even if he can't get their names straight. His tongue has a tendency to be as Dyslexic as his eyes.

"Oh babe, don't worry. I'll be careful this time," he promises me.

I hesitate for another instant, then hand him the packet while I get him a clean syringe from my bottomless purse. He goes into the bathroom, IV pole and all, and fixes. When he rejoins me in our makeshift bed, we turn on the TV and go back to snuggling.

But I can't get comfortable. No matter how I try I can no longer ignore how completely our world is falling apart. Bette's right, Steve and I are both dying. We're killing ourselves one high at a time.

Somehow, this doesn't much feel like recreation any more.

# CHAPTER EIGHT
## PEN PALS

*1984 through 1990*

Since the FBI took Terry off to jail our connection with our still BFF has been via the United States Post Office. It doesn't bother Terry that the FBI copies everything he sends to me and Steve. Nor does it bother him that all his phone calls are taped.

Terry's an excellent correspondent, although he tends to be fond of exclamation points. I receive something almost daily from him, letters, notes, cards. He's even written a manuscript, which he shared with me. It's a novel about the exploits of a hired hit man, no doubt drawn on Terry's personal experience as a hired hit man. It's some scary reading.

As for his letters, some are pretty mundane. Here's an excerpt from one he sent shortly after we ran away from Amity:

*Dear Monica,*
*I'm so glad you guys are home I could scream! Sure the program was cool but I like to see people be themselves!*

This doesn't mean Terry wasn't keen on us cleaning up. The opposite is true. His letters to me during my year in the program were wholly supportive of Steve and me kicking our habit. Frankly, we're a whole lot more useful to him clean and sober than as strung out junkies.

The letter goes on:

*And I know Mario is glad you are home!*

Mario lived with friends while we were away. Actually, Mario is really glad to be with us again, especially since we've moved to Tempe, Arizona and bought him a house with a pool. I think Mario likes swimming and lying out in the sun even more than I do.

> *Too bad I can't come now, we'd have a fucking*
> *party for 6 months! I mean that too. At least*
> *you'll get a chance to see Meatball!*

Meatball is Terry's pet name for his son by Debbie. Debbie is his third wife and was eighteen to Terry's thirty-eight when they married a few years back. It's in Debbie's interest to be a good wife to Terry; his previous two wives are dead. Terry doesn't do alimony.

> *And Monica you can drive up with Debbie some*
> *time and see me! That will be really fun. So*
> *please write and let me know if you all are*
> *gonna stay there etc. And get me a phone*
> *number. Even with my ten minutes a month*
> *call I'd like to talk to you! Nobody has been any*
> *more supportive then you all have with me.*

Fun. Hmm. That's right; I just love visiting maximum security prisons. As for supportive, I'm really glad Terry thinks that of me. It's just so much healthier that way.

Here's another letter, this one a little more chilling. It arrives after Terry has a falling out with one of our dearest friends in the Ghetto, Red, or Sekou, his Muslim name. Red is a fence and one of Terry's dealers. It was Red who introduced us to Terry, something no one could have imagined back when we first started buying our shit at Red's house.

When I say house, I mean the place from which Red sold drugs. Red has another house off Prospect Avenue where his wife and his children live. I only met her once or twice. She runs their restaurant and Sekou's Boutique, Red's store where, I assume, Red sells his fenced goods.

Red's drug house was in the hard-core heart of Kansas City's ghetto and we were pretty much the only Whities in his basement shooting gallery. It didn't make us popular. But Steve turned on the charm. Between that and Steve's willingness to loan Red money when his cash flow dried up, we were soon joining Red and his second-in-command Jamal upstairs.

Before long, we were all great friends. Jamal would entertain us with his jokes when the TV wasn't on. We even celebrated Christmas with them, arriving after leaving Ralph's and Mary Helen's house on Christmas Eve. Over the years, our celebration with Red developed nearly as many traditions as the ones that were part of the Sarlis' Italian fest. Every year, Steve would show Red the substantial check his father always gives him. Red would nod then let us buy our drugs with a promise to pay later in the week. Back then, there were no ATMS and the banks closed for the holidays.

After that, Steve would give Red his present, a case of Asti Spumante, Red's favorite wine. Of course, that meant they needed to open a bottle or two or three, with Steve, Jamal and Red all sharing, despite Red being Muslim. Not me. I don't care for the stuff.

By the way, neither Red nor Jamal ever used drugs. Not so, Zana, Red's mistress who lived at the drug house. We never got close to her; she was too paranoid, a condition I believe was caused by her drug use.

Anyway, in this letter Terry claims that Red has unofficially borrowed twenty thousand dollars from Terry's cash flow and hasn't yet paid it back:

> . . .I'm a very vindictive person! I never forget or forgive anyone! Who crosses me!. . .But her (meaning his wife Debbie) and Red are playing a little game with me it seems!. . .

Terry gets to the point a few paragraphs later:

> . . .Monica, I'll never lie to you. They trying to Hit Brother Red! Three Different groups of Dealers! So, just between you and me don't be with him and get hurt by accident! He knows already! I being a true friend warned him. Against everyone's wishes! So he knows! Now its on him to stay alive! Just you and Steve don't get caught near him. The Feds want to bust him, the crooks want to kill him! I know you like him, but restrain yourself, okay!. . .
>
> No doubt his phone is tapped. No calls from you! It's Best! Okay!...

Here's the translation from Drug Dealer to English: I've ordered Red to be hit, so for your own safety you and Steve better stay away from Kansas City and Red. And, don't you dare warn him about what I'm planning because I will know the warning came from you.

Terry is always encoding his letters to hide what he's doing from the FBI, but in this case he's just making sure he's clear to us because he'd really hate to hit us as well.

The letter continues for a few more pages with complaints about Debbie, worry over his son and for his brother Jerry, who is now incarcerated in Indiana and having health problems.

Terry signs it:

*Love Forever, Terry Kelton.*

Love Forever. Yikes. Just what I fucking need, Terry's eternal love.

Just as Terry warned, Red is hit a few weeks later in a typical gangland slaying. It happens sometime between three and five in the morning as Red is closing up his Prospect Avenue drug house. As Red steps outside to lock the door three guys in a car parked at the curb spray him with bullets.

Like I said, you don't mess with Terry and walk away unscathed.

We return to Kansas City to attend Red's funeral. Steve serves as one of the pallbearers. A handful of FBI agents also attend, no doubt cataloging the attendees. Red's obituary praises him as a generous man who took care of his neighbors as well as his own family, which he did.

What a conundrum. Drug dealer, man of the community, and they're both right.

After the funeral Terry sends us this letter, dated October 3, 1985:

*Dearest Monica,*

*I guess you are back now from KC. I heard it was a very short wake. Muslim by nature. I hate I wasn't there. Nobody was prepared! Too die. I also heard the wife and Zana are fighting already over the houses and property. But everything is in his wife's name. So she'll end up with it. But Zana bought it all for Red! Life is sort of unfair. However Zana can take care of herself and get more money. That ain't no problem at all. Seems we never*

*ready for People to Die!  Especially those close
to Us.  I want you to give me your word that
whenever I die you'll come to my funeral too.
That's all I want you to promise me Monica.
Don't get me wrong. I'm not planning on dying
anytime soon.  But nobody is Promised tomor
row.  We all know for a fact, it never would of
happened if I was home.  Hey did you and
Steve see Debbie at the Funeral?  She was so
tight with Red!  He owed her five thousand
dollars now that I think of it.  All debts are paid
when you die!  Monica I'm glad you are out
of that town and safe.  You and Steve need to
slow down a little.  I talked to a friend of mine
on the Phone!  And it's a lot of under current
out there.  People shifting weight for this.  My
name even came up.  I don't care what nobody
says.  But they will when I'm home.  Things
look really good now on my parole and the ap
peal for the DATE!  So I could be out early next
year maybe.  May 1986! I'm seriously planning
on moving up there by you guys.  I already
almost made up my mind.  At least I could
Legally change my name and live in Peace.
Ain't nothing on the Streets!  I'll be the rest of
my life trying to get Jerry out!  I don't need no
problems with the law.  Not at my age.  I got
to Raise Meatball and teach him.  I really want
to see you and Steve and Live where we can
see one another regularly. Be Good and Write!*
     *As Always, Love Terry Kelton.*
     *Give Steve my warmest regards.*

Well, fuck. Terry Kelton, my new neighbor.  That's really
something to look forward to.

89

# CHAPTER NINE
## DONE WITH IT

*August 4, 1986*
*Tempe, Arizona*

I wake with a start.  Steve's in bed beside me, snoring.  But that's not what woke me.

Something's changed.  I stare up at the vaulted ceiling above wondering what it is I'm feeling.

Mario's tail thumps on the plush carpeting from my side of the bed.  He always sleeps on the floor there.  I roll onto my side and reach for him.  He gets up and stretches with a groan, inviting me to give his ears a scratch.

As I do what he wants I look past him at the sitting room connected to our bedroom.  A beehive fireplace fills the wall across from me.  In front of it is a chair and ottoman upholstered in the same pink and gray fabric as my bedspread.  It's a beautiful space and I love everything about this bedroom, especially the big glass slider that leads out to our pool.  Outside the sun is just beginning to rise.  The pool tiles and water both gleam blue.

I sigh.  I love everything about this house.  Somehow, in thinking that I understand what woke me.

It's happened.  I'm done with drugs.  I know to the

core of my bones that I can't take it anymore. I won't take it anymore.

I want to be clean like I've never before wanted anything.

That brings me up onto one elbow so I can look down at my husband. My waist length hair slides forward until strands drape across Steve's face.

I give him a shake. "Wake up."

"What is it?" Steve groans, brushing my hair off his face.

He squints up at me. He looks like shit. His skin is sallow. His hair is greasy.

"I'm done, Steve," I announce.

He stares blearily at me then loses his focus and starts to slip back toward sleep. We haven't been in bed that long. As his expression relaxes, I notice the wrinkles at the corners of his eyes don't disappear like they used to. He's aged over the past months, especially since his overdose. It makes me wonder if it's aged me as well.

I know I feel like I'm ancient. My mind fills with the images of all the toothless, drugged out and eaten up addicts I've ever met, and I've met a lot of them. Oh God, I don't want to end up looking like them.

"What do you mean, you're done?" he murmurs, eyes closed.

"I'm finished using. No more drugs. I want to be clean again," I tell him, then add, "You too."

Steve not cleaning up isn't an option. I know I can't have Heroin in the house if I'm not using. I also know I can't live with a drinking Steve without Heroin to keep him mellow. Since I'm not giving up Steve, he has to clean up with me.

That startles him back to almost full consciousness. Although his eyes don't open, his jaw tightens in resistance. I read his mind.

"Not Amity," I assure him. "I'm going to find a Methadone clinic. You're coming with me, right?'

He opens one eye to look at me, then inhales, long and deep. "Okay," he says, scrubs a hand over his face, rolls onto his side with his back to me and pulls the blanket around his shoulders. "Whatever you want is okay with me."

I guess I shouldn't be surprised by his agreement. First, Steve's always been a real get along sort of guy. Unless he's been drinking, he'll agree to anything rather than fight. More importantly, if I stop buying Steve's drugs for him he'd have to start buying his own and that's not in Steve's job description.

As for me, I don't care why he agrees only that he has. I put a hand on his shoulder, listening as his breathing slows and lengthens. He's asleep again. Not me. I can't wait to start my new life.

I get up and scour the Yellow Pages for our nearest private Methadone treatment center. I find one located not too far from our house. It's not open on Sundays, so I can't start my new life until Monday at six in the morning when it opens.

Having committed myself to a new sober life, what do I do next? Why, I go out into the hundred degree plus day, find Luis, make my last drug buy, then Steve and I party for as much of the next twenty-four hours as our stash allows.

Then right at six the next morning, I cart Steve down to the clinic. It feels like heaven when I sign myself in for treatment.

Methadone and Heroin produce very similar highs. The only difference is that one is legal and the other is not. The correct way to use Methadone is to take it at my typical Heroin dosage so I can wean myself off Heroin without withdrawal symptoms. The tricky part is to then wean myself off Methadone.

"The ideal outcome," says Dr. Richard Musco, the doctor who runs the clinic, "is for you two to leave the clinic addiction free. Of course," he continues, "that isn't something every addict is capable of doing, especially addicts with as long a history of Heroin usage as the two of you."

He pauses to glance between us. He's a handsome man, with a full head of dark hair and a fondness for Italian shoes. Steve and I sit in his private office for this, our first consult. The sound of rush hour traffic is louder than the sound of the air conditioner running at high. It's already over a hundred outside even this early.

"But many addicts find they can live perfectly normal lives, hold down good jobs and raise their families, while continuing to use Methadone."

I look at him. Unless I kick Methadone after I kick Heroin I'll always be just a few legal doses away from falling back into my original addiction. Nor is being forever tied to this clinic and my new legal drug what I want for me and Steve.

"I don't care how long it takes or how many surprise urine tests it requires. I don't even care that the red goop you mix with the Methadone always makes me gag." I call the stuff Cool-ade even though it tastes nothing like the sweet drink I had as a kid. This tastes more like nasty Cherry cough syrup to me. "This time we're going all the way," I pronounce. I am determined the day will come when we will both be completely drug free. "Right, Steve?"

Steve grins, but it looks more like a grimace this morning. We're pretty strung out. "Right," he agrees.

"Good for you," the doctor says, then fills out the forms to calculate our starting dosage. He looks up at us. "I just want you to be aware that this is a pretty high dosage. We don't usually see addicts with as long a usage as yours."

What he means is that people who use at our level for as long as we have are usually dead by now.

So, we start drinking the cough syrup. 1986 becomes 1987. I swear I can tell each time my dosage is reduced. All of a sudden I have all those familiar Flu-like symptoms I experienced each time I went cold turkey. My muscles ache, my stomach gets upset and those awful Heroin sweats start up. The average time it takes to overcome the physical effects of Heroin leaving the body is seventy-two hours and that's exactly how long these symptoms last.

1987 turns into 1988. As two years of using Methadone becomes three, I persist to my goal of drug free or bust. Steve and I will not become the old couple I see at the clinic from time to time. They've been on Methadone for ten plus years. I refuse to live out the rest of my life this way. This clinic is as much a prison as the one that continues to refuse to release Terry Kelton.

*July, 1989*
*Tempe, Arizona*

It's six o'clock in the fucking morning and I'm barely coherent as I stand at the waiting room counter in our Methadone clinic. Steve stands next to me, looking far more chipper. I am not a morning person, but Steve likes coming to the clinic when it first opens. He doesn't like being here when the waiting room is crowded. He says he doesn't like looking at *those* people. He means the other addicts, some of whom are really down and out even though this is a more upscale clinic.

This has been our routine for the past three years, although when we started we were coming daily. After three years of clean urine tests, they now trust us enough to let us take two days' worth of Methadone home with us. That means we're here Monday, Wednesday and Friday. We've also gained the ability to take the occasional vacation as long as it lasts no longer than ten days; that's as much Methadone as the clinic is legally allowed to give us at any one time.

Vacations are one of the most surprising things to come out of cleaning up. Prior to this, we didn't travel. Even if we'd wanted to, we couldn't have. As long as we needed a steady supply of illicit drugs to keep us going, we sure as fuck weren't going to go gallivanting around the world, hoping and praying we'd find a dealer somewhere along the way. Pasta conventions don't really count as vacations, even if they're held in really nice places. Like I said, there's too much pressure, everyone sneaking around, listening in on each other's conversations, trying to figure out what the hot new pasta shape is going to be.

So, along with Methadone came vacations. Our first one was a cruise, mostly because we were overwhelmed by our choices. It seemed a lot easier to get on board a ship and let it make the choices for us. We've been in love with big boats from that first day at sea.

Nurse Bonnie smiles at us the way she does every morning and comes to stand across the counter from us. She's pretty, dark-haired and friendly. Over the past three years she and I have become friends. I've even been to her house for a Tupperware party.

"Morning, Steve. Monica," she says to us.

"Morning, honey," Steve tells her, all grins and twinkles. All the women who cross Steve's and Ralph's paths are either honeys or sweethearts. I'm Steve's only babe.

"Hey Bonnie," I manage. I'm just awake enough to realize there's something different about her this morning. I watch as Bonnie flips through the patient list on her clipboard as if she's looking for our names and dosages. What? Like she doesn't know them by now?

I'm just about ready to ask her what's going on when she holds up our paperwork. "Here it is. Good news," she says, her grin broad and pleased. "No more Methadone for you two."

"What?" Steve asks.

"What?" I echo, stunned. "What do you mean, no more Methadone?"

"I mean you're done," Bonnie says. "You guys have been drinking nothing but your syrup for the past six weeks. You're done. You're clean, just like you said you'd be."

Her words hit me like a blow. My legs feel like wet noodles. My vision dims for just a second as my head spins.

Bonnie comes out from behind the counter and puts her

arms around me to give me a hug. I fall gratefully into her embrace. I swear I'd be laying flat out on the floor if not for it.

"Congratulations, Monica. I knew you'd do it," she tells me as she releases me. Her dark eyes glow with pride. "We're all so proud of you, aren't we?" she calls to the rest of the office staff. They're all gathered on the far side of the counter, watching. At her prod, they offer us their congratulations.

I'm still struggling to take it in. After almost a lifetime of using mind-altering drugs, after three years of using legal drugs, I'm finally, truly clean and sober.

Bonnie releases me, leaving me to stagger drunkenly until I'm leaning against the counter, and goes to Steve. She offers him a hug as well. "Congratulations, Steve."

Steve turns it into a bear hug, lifting the small woman off her feet. "We're done!" he laughs, his proclamation ringing like a shout in the small room. He sets Bonnie's feet back on the floor then grins down at her. "No offense honey, but I won't miss you."

"None taken," she replies. "But I will miss you two."

That's when the enormity of our accomplishment finally hits me. We're free. Steve and I never ever have to come back here.

Tears spring to my eyes. No more getting up at five so Steve and I can be the first patients in the door each morning, or carting around coolers filled with Methadone. No more crackpot ideas about using Heroin on the weekends. No more chasing down a drug dealer, even legal ones with medical degrees. I will never again have to worry when someone asks me to pee in a cup. I will never again have to lie to my family or Steve's when they ask me if I'm sober.

And in this instant I know I will be sober from this day forward without fail. For the rest of my life I will honor the promise I made myself three years ago on August fourth. I am done with drugs.

Steve starts laughing. He holds his fists high and does a little dance. "We are the champions," he gloats happily. "We're done! We never have to come back here," he announces to the few folks in the waiting room.

Laughing, I throw myself into Steve's arms. "Let's go out to breakfast to celebrate."

Going out to eat isn't exactly special for us. Like Mary Helen, I'm not Steve's chef. Not that I can't cook. Steve's just used to his family's routine of eating out more than eating in. We always go out after visiting the clinic, though, because doughnuts went a long way to masking the syrup's taste. Because this morning is really special we go to The Waffle House. It's Belgian Waffles all around.

Our elation is just beginning to ebb as Steve and I return home. Then it's time to return to our normal lives, no matter how strange it feels to do so today. That means Steve goes into his home office to work.

Steve formed a company not long ago called Emerald Coast Financial. It's in the business of financing real estate development projects around Arizona as well as investing in the stock market. I'm vice president. Cushiest job I've ever had since I don't have to actually do anything. And, I can't beat the hours, as in none. Steve's funding it with the new money that's come his way.

A few months ago, Grand Met, a British conglomerate, purchased Pillsbury for a whole lotta cash. Because of the stock exchange arrangement Ralph negotiated between American Beauty and Pillsbury all those years ago, this new sale resulted in a few more millions being deposited in Steve's trust account, the one Ralph had him set up thirteen years ago. Until the trust finally opens in 1991, the money sits there generating interest, which Steve can use as he pleases.

I drift into our bedroom to lie on the bed and watch TV. Only then does the reality of this day finally hit me full force. Oh. My. Fucking. God.

I can't have any more Methadone.

Panic rises like a tidal wave. I'm not ready. I know I don't want to do Heroin or drink. But how am I going to manage without my daily dose of Methadone?

Just like that my muscles start to ache. I shiver, suddenly freezing, and try to reach for the blanket. There's not an iota of energy left in me. It takes all my will just to sit up. Even my hair starts to hurt.

Oh the power of words. I'm in full withdrawal mode, only today I'm withdrawing from the Methadone that I haven't had for six weeks. Oh fuck, does this mean I'm not going to be able to sleep for the next seventy-two hours fifteen minutes and twenty-two seconds, the way I never could when I'd try withdrawing cold turkey from Heroin?

My first impulse is to call to Steve and tell him what I'm feeling. I stifle it. I don't want to put ideas into his head. What if I tell him and it triggers him to want to use again? I want to be strong for both of us.

The panic persists. Just like my other withdrawals, I drop into a fitful doze. When I wake, Steve is lying on the bed beside me watching TV. "Oh baby," I say. "I'm not feeling too good. How do you feel?"

Steve looks at me. I can see it in his eyes. He's feeling the same thing I am. "I don't feel very good either," he admits. "But I'm sure it will pass."

I nod. Yeah, right. It'll pass, in seventy-two hours.

It actually only takes me about thirty hours to withdraw from the idea of no more drugs, but when it's over I wake up and feel fine. No, I feel stunned, happy, proud, alive, but mostly I feel clean and sober.

It also occurs to me that I've just recovered my way out of my job in our marriage, that of maintaining our relationship with our dealers and/or recovery doctors. So, what am I going to do now?

I'm still savoring the exhilaration of my accomplishment a few days later when a tall, black, very official looking man appears at my door. He shows me his badge. Officer Thurman, it says. He's a federal parole officer.

My heart sinks. That can only mean one thing: Terry Kelton.

In every one of Terry's letters these past few months he's talked about how he's now served almost all of the time required to satisfy his parole violation. However, the authorities won't release him if he can't find some solid, stable never-been-convicted-of-anything citizen to sponsor him. They're pretty bald hints that he wants Steve and me to be his sponsors.

Neither of us ever told him we would do it. Then again, we also never told him we wouldn't do it. We didn't think we'd ever have to confront the issue. Apparently, Terry took our non-agreement to be consent. Then again, I doubt our agreement matters to Terry.

Up until about two seconds ago Terry's potential release was just a distant cloud on my horizon, one I've pretty much managed to ignore.

Isn't that in the Serenity Prayer? . . .*grant to me the serenity to accept what cannot be changed; to ignore what I can't do anything about. . .*

I suppose not.

Although Terry always insisted that the FBI wouldn't be able to charge him for his fire sale drug ring, I didn't believe it. It's the fucking FBI. I was sure they'd find a way to keep him in jail. After all, everyone else who worked in that ring, including Gilbert Dowdy the fire chief has been arrested. Not Terry. And no one's even talking about all those bodies in Swope Park Lake. The only thing keeping Terry in jail is his parole violation.

Now it looks like Terry knows best.

Since Officer Thurman seems nice enough, I let him in. As I lead him into the living room of our Tempe house, he scans my professionally decorated home. I love our decorator, Carol Minchew. She gave us arches, neutral colors and interesting furniture, and became my friend.

The good officer and I sit then he looks at me in confusion. "How the hell did Terry Kelton get someone like you to sponsor him?"

"So, he's really getting out?" I ask, praying Officer Thurman will throw me a line because I'm drowning in despair.

It doesn't happen. Instead, Officer Thurman cheerfully informs me, "He's almost completed all the time he needs to do for his parole violation. It could happen any time in the next six months."

Once again, he stops and stares at me. "I gotta ask. How do you know him?"

There's nothing for me to do but run my story to the nice officer. That's Amity-speak for making sure I tell the whole and complete truth about my past. Running my story is one of Amity's three principles for living a sober life. They are: Never Lie, Help Others, and Always Run Your Story. Just because I didn't stay at Amity long enough to graduate doesn't mean I didn't learn anything. I want to make sure I forever remain sober.

This morning I admit I was an addict for years and that Terry was my dealer. I also tell Officer Thurman Steve and I have just completed and been released from our Methadone program, that we're clean now. I couldn't have said that last week. I even tell him that Terry's been nothing but supportive of my recovery.

I don't include the information that Terry considers me and Steve his closest friends.

When I finish Officer Thurman closes his notebook. He smiles at me. "I can't see any reason you wouldn't be perfect sponsors for Mr. Kelton. And I want to add that you're doing a wonderful thing for him. I can't think of many people in your situation who'd be willing to do something like this."

I smile weakly back at him. Fuck, fuck, fuck! Terry's about to escape his life sentence, but I'm still doing life with Terry. And I have absolutely no hope of parole.

# CHAPTER TEN
# WITNESS
# PROTECTION?

*November 24, 1989*
*Thanksgiving Weekend*
*Kansas City, Missouri*

As usual, Steve and I are spending our holiday in Kansas City. These days instead of staying with Ralph and Mary Helen we stay at a hotel. For this trip it's a room at the Westin Hotel. We started doing this as part of our recovery in the Methadone program. We want to—need to—avoid the drinking at the Sarli house. That, and ever since Steve's been sober he's more comfortable keeping a little space between him and his father.

Yesterday was Thanksgiving, so I'm taking it easy in the hotel room while Steve and his dad have breakfast at the Plaza. The phone rings. It's Mary Helen.

"Are Steve and Ralph back yet?" She sounds strange, more strained than usual.

"Not yet. What's up?" I ask her.

"Um, there were just two FBI agents at the door. They're looking for you and Steve," Mary Helen tells me.

The FBI? This can only be about Terry Kelton. I think. I hope?

With new urgency in her voice, Mary Helen adds,

"What's going on? Are you two using drugs again? Are you in trouble?"

"Mary Helen, we're clean." Even four months after completing the program, pride fills me as I say those two little words. I absolutely love not having to lie about my sobriety or what Steve and I are doing. My exhilaration is followed by a satisfying sense of accomplishment. I hope I never stop being thrilled about living a clean and sober life.

There's silence on the other end of the line. It's filled with the sound of Mary Helen's doubts. I don't blame her. Steve and I have lied to her so many times in the past. It may take her a long while to trust us again.

"Honestly, Mary Helen," I assure her. "We aren't using."

"Well, as soon as Steve gets back I think you need to get over here," she says, all business now. "I told them you'd be at the house later today. They really want to see you."

I hang up, uncertain whether I should worry or hope.

Steve barely gets inside the hotel room before I'm all over him.

"Steve, FBI agents were just at your parents' house looking for us."

He stops where he stands, his eyes wide. "Oh shit." I watch as the same uncertainty I feel shows on his face. He rubs a hand across his brow. "What do you think, babe? Terry Kelton?"

"Who else?" I reply. "What should we do?"

He shrugs. "What can we do? It's the FBI. We have to talk to them."

As eager as I am to keep Terry from living with me, I'm not certain I want to talk to the FBI here in our hotel room. I know I don't want to talk to them in their office. That would feel as if I was putting myself completely into their hands and that doesn't sit well.

"What do you think?" I ask. "Should we blow them off until we get home?"

"No way," Steve interrupts. "We're doing this right now and we're doing it at my parents' house."

I almost sigh in relief. Steve's exactly right. What we need now is the security of Ralph's prestige and power wrapped around us.

We jump into our rental car. As we make the quick drive to his parents' house I stare out the car window. It's November and all the trees and lawns all look dead, as dead as I'll be if I end up in prison.

The thought comes out of nowhere, startling me. For what?

How about trafficking in narcotics, for starters?

I shake off the thought. I refuse to let this interview be about anything I've done. The only thing the FBI's ever been interested in is keeping Terry, and that's what this will be about as well.

Besides, having to go to prison after I worked so hard to free Steve and me from our addictions and our past just wouldn't be fair.

Steve parks the car in front of his parents' home. Ralph must have been watching from the window, because the garage door opens for us. The inner garage door takes us into their family room. The bar, their altar to alcohol, is on our right. To the left of the door is Ralph's built-in desk. He sits in his well used yellow leather desk chair, which is where he sits each and every night as he and Mary Helen share their cocktails. Mary Helen is not far from Ralph, sitting in her time-honored place: the little chair that faces the bay window. Although they've obviously been waiting for us to arrive, there's no expression on their faces as they watch us come in.

Their concern may not be expressed, but I know them well enough to read beneath the surface. Whatever the FBI might want, Ralph and Mary Helen will see to it Steve and I are safe. In that instant I love them both. They're doing all they can to protect us any way they can, no matter what we may or may not have done.

"What's going on?" Ralph demands as the door closes behind me.

"We don't know," I reply for both Steve and me. We might have cleaned up, but it's still my job to speak for Steve.

"They left a number for you to call." Ralph takes a slip of paper off his desk and hands it to me.

Of course he does. Some things never change. Steve will always be Ralph's helpless little screw up and I'll always be Ralph's Cleaner when it comes to taking care of Steve.

I start for the kitchen to make the call. To my surprise, Steve follows me rather than staying in the family room with his parents. His support makes it a lot easier to dial the number on the note.

A man answers, spitting out his name in harsh syllables.

"Hi, this is Monica Sarli," I say.

I barely get my name out before he's speaking over me. "Thanks for calling. We need to talk. When can we meet?"

"Steve and I are here at Ralph Sarli's house," I tell him.

"Our agents will be right there," he says, then practically drops the phone.

And the agents are right there. They arrive so quickly I wonder if they weren't parked somewhere nearby, waiting for my call. Or maybe watching the house. Or maybe waiting in the bushes. That's how swiftly they arrived.

I open the door for them. Steve and Ralph are at my back.

Agent One introduces himself as Jerry. He seems nice enough, smiling and friendly, an average looking guy. There's nothing about him that suggests he's any sort of threat to Steve and me.

Agent Two is an equally average looking guy, although bigger and his expression is colder as he eyes us with some calculation and no smiles.

Ralph glares at the agents, watching as Steve and I shake their hands. "So what's this about?" he asks gruffly.

"We really need to speak to Monica and Steve alone," Jerry says, still all smiles. "Is there someplace private where we can talk to them?"

I can see the agent's words don't sit well with Ralph. "Do I need to call my attorney and get him over here?" He wants the agents to know from the get-go they aren't dealing with just anybody in this house, they're dealing with Ralph Sarli.

"There's no need for that," Jerry replies, taking Ralph's hostility in stride. "This won't take too long."

His partner remains silent.

Ralph looks at me and Steve. He's worried. But I'm not willing to put this off.

We're not doing drugs. We haven't done anything illegal lately. And I want to know what they want.

"We'll be okay," I tell Ralph.

"Fine." Ralph grudgingly points toward the stairway that leads down to their Rec Room.

This is the room they use when throwing large parties. It's tastefully decorated with thick shag carpeting, light wood wainscoting and off-white walls. A comfy overstuffed couch and several heavy rattan chairs with a matching table between them are arranged near a brick fireplace. This is where Steve and I used to make out when we were dating. Ralph's antique slot machine is placed at the base of the stairs, while a much bigger bar than the one upstairs lines the opposite wall. The barstools are in the old style, with a pedestal base and a round leather seat.

French doors offer an expansive view of their small patio that gives way to their open and grassy backyard. Their yard rolls all the way down to State Line Road. There's no fence to block our view of the neighbor's house. The Sarlis have very nice neighbors. Her family once owned Peabody Coal.

Steve and I take the couch—old habits die hard—while Agent Jerry and his partner take the chairs. We're having our own fireside chat here.

Jerry starts. "We appreciate you taking time to talk to us. I'm sure you're wondering why we're here. Terry Kelton is scheduled to be released this December."

December?! That's only days away. My heart starts to pound. I can't stop the image of Terry living in my guest room and me cooking—both food and Crack Cocaine—for him.

"I don't know if you're aware that we've been watching Terry Kelton closely for the last seven years," he continues.

Steve shoots me a sidelong glance, the quirk of his eyebrow saying: Does he really think we're that stupid?

Now, Agent Jerry's expression hardens. He shifts back in his chair, his arms crossed in refusal. "He's not getting out and he will no longer be able to run his Cocaine operation from prison. It's time for that to stop."

I'm dizzy in relief as the weight of the world lifts off my shoulders. No Terry in my guest room. No threat to my sobriety.

Steve combs his fingers through his hair, and then rubs his face with his hands. These are things he does only when he's nervous. "That's great news, but what does it have to do with us?"

"We know through all of Kelton's phone calls and letters to you that you two, especially Monica, are very close to Kelton. For some reason, he's let you into his life. He obviously trusts you and that's not normal for him," Agent Jerry says.

I think what he means is that it's not normal behavior for most murdering psychopaths to keep best friends.

Jerry continues. "We are getting ready to indict him at this moment on twenty-nine counts ranging from drug dealing to murder. But if this is going to happen, we need your help."

I'm stunned. I look at Steve and he's as flabbergasted

as I am. The FBI needs our help?

"What can we do?" I ask.

"We need your cooperation. We need you both to testify against Kelton and his organization."

"Oh my God, we can't do that," I blurt out. Fuck me. I can't betray Terry. He trusts me.

"You need to," Agent Jerry replies, his tone almost that of pleading. "All our other witnesses are either junkies or felons with rap sheets the length of your arm. Without your testimony, we're afraid Kelton will go free."

"And if we don't?" Steve demands. He's moved forward in his chair, his chest thrust out in what I know is bravado.

"We will indict you both for trafficking narcotics and for wiring money for illegal purposes over state lines, which is a federal offense." It's Jerry's erstwhile silent partner who speaks this time and his threat hangs like icicles from his lips. He stares at us, as if he's looking forward to putting us in prison.

I feel like I've been sucker punched. I can't catch my breath. Oh fuck.

Not too long ago a small box with eleven thousand dollars in it appeared on my doorstep via a ground carrier. Terry called shortly afterward and asked if I'd received his package. When I said I had, he instructed me to keep a thousand of it as payment for my assistance in the matter and wire the other ten thousand to one of the men who ran some of Terry's Crack houses.

I did what Terry asked because I always do what Terry asks. I did it even though I knew it was wrong when I did it. That's how Life with Terry works.

"You'll also have to appear before a grand jury to testify about your involvement with Kelton," Jerry finishes, his tone softer, less threatening.

All my hopes for our future, for any future at all, dissolve. I swear I hear the echo of a prison door slamming. My heart starts doing an awful little shuck and jive. I curl my fingers to keep them from shaking.

I can't go to prison. I won't. Chances are prison life is a lot like life at Amity, and I didn't do really well in that environment. If I go to prison, will Mary Helen send me my Lancôme products the way she did while I was at Amity?

Steve leaps to his feet, his fists balled and his face red. "This meeting's over and I need to call my attorney."

He reaches down and takes my hand. His fingers tighten on mine to urge me to stand with him.

"There's no need to do that, Steve," Jerry says again gently, trying to calm the situation. "Just sit down. We'll talk this thing out."

I don't know why, but what Jerry says causes something to resonate within in me. The sensation grows until it washes over me like a tidal wave. My attachment to Terry isn't a friendship, it's an addiction.

The gangster life, the drugs, the Ghetto, all the stories, all the murders, they're all just another drug I use to alter my reality. If I'm honest with myself I have to admit that even reading Terry's letters about my former life gives me an adrenaline rush. That's not living sober.

If I truly want to shut the door on my past, I have no choice but to leave Terry there in it.

And the only way to shut that door and have the clean and sober future I want is to help the FBI destroy Terry, no matter how much it hurts me to do it.

Steve tugs on my hand again. I still don't come to my feet. He glances down at me and frowns. I give a tiny shake of my head.

"Babe, trust me," I say softly to him, stroking Steve's hand a little as I try to calm him. "Everything's going to be okay."

Steve stares at me like he's trying to read my mind. I can see that more than anything he wants to run upstairs and put all of this into Ralph's powerful and capable hands. But Ralph can't help us end our relationship with Terry.

"Steve," I whisper. "Please sit down. We need to listen to them. We need to do this."

The resistance drains from him. With a huff, he drops to sit beside me once again.

Jerry smiles at us. "Thank you, Steve. And you, Monica. We really appreciate your patience and what you're doing here.

"So, why don't you tell us from the beginning. How did you meet Terry Kelton? Just briefly. Tell us about you and Terry."

In my hurry to reach my future I almost vomit words, giving Jerry and his partner the Reader's Digest Condensed version of Life with Terry.

Steve lets me do most of the talking, just adding a few of the details I skip.

When we're done Agent Jerry nods. "Everything you've said agrees with what we know. Good. You're telling the truth. You do know that we have files on both of you? That all of your conversations with Kelton have been taped?"

Still giddy with relief, I almost laugh. Lucky them. Terry's conversations are pretty boring. Like his letters, his calls to me are mostly complaints about Debbie doing him and Meatball wrong.

"We also have copies of all his letters to you," he adds.

Again, Steve and I exchange glances. Does he think we missed that Terry's letters arrived taped shut? I pity the poor schmuck who had to do the copying. He must have worn out a machine duplicating Terry's copious letters.

"There's something we need to clear up. Tell us about Maurice."

His comment takes me aback. It was Maurice who received the ten thousand dollars Terry asked me to send. I liked Maurice. He was no killer like Terry, just a small, happy-go-lucky Crack distributer who dressed like Shaft. Then Terry started complaining about Maurice taking him for a fool. Not too long ago Maurice died the same way Red had. Zana,

Red's former mistress, called me to let me know.

"What about him?" I ask, suddenly nervous.

"Did you put out the hit on Maurice?" Jerry asks us, his expression flat.

Instantly and without looking at each other, Steve and I both break into laughter. The idea is so bizarre neither of us can imagine that they're serious.

Neither agent cracks a smile. Our laughter dies. They aren't joking.

"That's the word on the street, that you had him hit when he didn't repay you the money you loaned him," Agent Jerry continues.

"That's crazy! We didn't have anyone killed," Steve says, shaking his head in disbelief, "especially not Maurice. We liked Maurice."

To my surprise, Jerry says, "We believe you. We're just trying to get the story straight."

Now he leans forward, looking earnest and all-American in that FBI sort of way. "You've been amazingly helpful."

Steve glances at me before looking back at Jerry. "So, where do we go from here? What happens now?"

"We'll be calling you to testify to the grand jury about Kelton. Now that we've got credible witnesses, there can be a court trial."

That panic hits again. "Is Terry going to be in court?" I gasp out. I can't imagine having to face Terry from the witness box, not because he frightens me, which he does, but because he's my friend.

"I can't testify against him if he's there. He trusts me. I can't sit in a courtroom with him there and betray him. It would kill me to do that."

"Hmm," Jerry says, the sound his only acknowledgment of my pain. "The possibility of your demise brings us to another point. It's time to talk about putting you into the Witness Protection Program."

Agent Jerry's tone suggests they're already concocting

our new identities.

"You've got to be kidding me," I say in complete disbelief.

"No way," Steve says at the same time. "We're not moving and we're not changing our names."

Agent Jerry's silent partner again stirs himself. "You have no choice. Kelton will have you killed when he learns you're talking to us and planning to testify against him." He speaks slowly, as if dealing with folks who aren't quite up to par in the brains department.

"He's right. You won't be safe once Kelton learns we've talked to you. We need to keep you safe. You have to be able to testify," Agent Jerry adds hastily.

That gives me a flash of just how desperate they are to recruit us as their star witnesses.

"No." Steve comes to his feet and this time I stand with him. "No Witness Protection."

"Absolutely not," I agree. "We're not going into your program."

Jerry and his partner also stand. It looks like our friendly little chat is at an end. And, really, it has been friendly. Even Agent Iceman's threats have been made in the most pleasant manner.

They really, really need us.

"Before we leave, you should understand that it would be in your best interest to have no further contact with Kelton," Jerry says.

That makes me laugh. "Easy for you to say. You know, you've spent all this time listening to us talk on the phone and you still don't get it, do you? Come Monday morning, Terry's going to call me at home and ask how our holiday went in Kansas City. Just the tone of my voice will tell him that something's wrong, because that's how well he knows me. You better believe that when he asks what's wrong, I'm going to tell him about this meeting. I'm not going to tell him about it to expose your investigation, I'm going to do it because, first, I wouldn't be surprised if he already knows you're here today," I tell Agent Jerry and mean it. "And, second, I'll tell him because I am always completely honest with Terry Kelton."

"That could be dangerous," Jerry replies, but I shake my head.

"No offense, but I'll put my trust in Terry Kelton before the FBI." I never again lied to Terry after that little incident with the Cocaine.

Standing in the Sarlis' basement, Iceman and Jerry stare at us for a long moment. Both of them shake their heads. I can see it in their eyes. They're convinced that we're either nuts or have death wishes.

Steve and I let the agents start up the stairs ahead of us. A few steps up Iceman stops and turns.

"Oh, one last thing. If you don't mind, there's some code in Kelton's letters to you we haven't been able to decipher."

"Like what?" Steve asks.

Terry's code is so basic I can't believe there's anything the FBI can't figure out. Downtown refers to Junior Bradley, Terry's connection to Nick Civella. When Terry talked about fire sales, he was talking about Kansas City's fire chief and sales manager of the Terry Kelton Rock of the Day Club.

"Who is Mario?" Iceman asks.

I stare at the two of them. They must be kidding. How can they know so much, but still miss something so obvious?

"Mario's our dog."

"No way," he retorts, looking honestly surprised.

"Ask my in-laws if you don't believe us," I say. "Terry loves Mario."

Oh yeah, my trust is so much better placed in Terry than in guys who can't add one and one to come up with two.

That's when I see how this is going to all fall in place for me and Steve. I'm certain Terry already knows what's going down; Terry always knows what's happening, no matter what prison he's in or how tightly the authorities try to hold him. If that's so, then he also knows the Feds have what they need to force Steve and me to testify. I know just how my Monday morning conversation with Terry is going to go.

Our chummy little group reaches the top of the stairs. Agent Jerry and his partner shake our hands then open the door. Jerry smiles at us. "We'll be talking to you soon," he says.

Once the door closes behind them, I look at Ralph. "We need a lawyer," I say.

By the end of the day Steve and I have hired a friend of Ralph's, Jim Cashion. He'd once been head of the special government unit prosecuting organized crime in Kansas City. Luckily for us he's retired from government work and is in private practice representing the criminals he used to prosecute.

Not that we're criminals. At least not any more.

He assures us that there's no way we're going to prison, then goes off to chat with his friends in the FBI's local office. When he returns a few hours later it's with bad news for Steve and me. We really are the only credible witnesses the FBI has against Terry. Everyone else is either a down-at-the-heels junkie or a multi-charged criminal. Moreover, the Feds are holding firm. Terry won't be leaving prison and returning to his Kansas City operation because we're too scared to speak up. So far Jim's earning his retainer. He got his contacts to drop our appearance before the Grand Jury and delayed our first interview with the FBI's attorneys until mid-December. Until then, Steve and I are free to go.

This plan of mine had better work.


Just as I told Agent Jerry, bright and early on Monday morning the phone rings. It's Terry, calling collect of course.

"How are you?  How was Thanksgiving in Kansas City?"

"I've had better," I say.  "We've got a little problem.  The FBI came by the Sarlis' house while we were visiting."

Terry sighs.  There's a world of disappointment in the sound.  "I guess I'm not surprised.  I had a feeling they didn't want me getting out.  So what happened?"

"You know they're probably taping this?"

He laughs a little.  "Yeah."

"Well, they asked me not to talk to you, but I said we were friends.  They have everything, Terry, all the scoop on Gilbert Dowdy, on Red and about Maurice.  Twenty-nine counts in all.  Witnesses, too."

"Yeah, I know.  I'm fucked," Terry says flatly.

"So are we.  We have to go back in December to talk to them.  We have to agree to testify or they're going to put us in prison.  You can't imagine how upset our families are."

"Shit!  Steve's dad?  I'm so sorry."

Terry worries about our friendship with him making Steve look bad in Ralph's eyes.  That story about Steve's godfather still has him believing there's a connection between Ralph and Nick Civella.

I take a deep breath and jump into the deep end, hoping what I'm about to attempt will work.  If it doesn't, I'm not just fucked, I'll probably die in prison.

"Terry, I can't perjure myself and they have a lot of evidence.  You know I wouldn't do anything to hurt you.  You were so supportive of me getting off drugs.  I couldn't have done it without your love, support and friendship, but I can't go to prison.  You know me.  I won't do well with the food and the clothes.  It just won't work for me.  But that's where I'll be if I don't testify.

"Worse, the Feds are insisting that Steve and I go into the Witness Protection program.  They say you'll kill us.  Having to change our names and give up our families is worse than going to prison.  It would kill Ralph to lose Steve again, especially now that we're clean.  Terry, I have to testify.  I won't tell them anything they don't already know."

I pause for a swift breath then launch into the most important words I've ever spoken. "Are you going to kill me?"

"Of course I'm not going kill you," Terry replies. Although his voice is no more or less flat and cold than always, there's a hint of honesty and assurance in his tone.

I don't stop to think that I might be hearing it because that's what I want to hear. All I know is that Terry is making me a promise. I leap for the brass ring.

"I was hoping that's what you'd say. You know, I told the Feds that I'd take my chances with you because I trust you as a friend. I don't trust the FBI."

Silence follows. It's funny what quiet can impart on a phone. I swear I hear the tiny curl of lip that passes for a smile on Terry. Oddly enough, I'm glad I've pleased him.

"I'm only sorry that they're coming for you because of me," he tells me. "I never meant to embarrass you or your family." We chat until Terry's time is up.

When I put the receiver back on the cradle I'm absolutely certain that my cell door is open. Once the trial is over.

We meet with the FBI in December and Jerry informs us Terry has been moved to Leavenworth and is now in solitary. "Kelton won't be able to get to anyone ever again," he adds proudly.

That makes me laugh. "If you believe that, you're a fool. Terry will do what he wants no matter where you put him."

He looks insulted. Doesn't matter. I'm right.

Two months later in February 1990 I receive a Hallmark birthday card from Terry. There's only one way Terry could have signed a Hallmark card in his prison cell: one of his guards went to the store and bought it for him.

I call Agent Jerry. "I just want you to know Terry's shopping at Hallmark. That's why I wasn't going into your Witness Protection Program. Like I said, Terry does what he wants."

Poor guy. He's stunned. But that's Terry. He's got some real leadership skills. People naturally do what he asks.

Terry calls me in the spring. By then the case, which has so far resulted in the indictment of more than half of Terry's organization, is on the docket. We're scheduled to go to trial in August.

"I'm pleading *Nolo Contendere*," Terry tells me. "That way I avoid the death penalty and I won't have to go to court."

"Good. That means I won't have to point to you while I'm on the stand. That would kill me," I reply, every word the truth.

"Yeah, me too," he says. "I don't think I could bear having to watch you on the stand while those clowns are asking you questions about me and my business. Just know that no one will hurt you because of what you do or say in court. No one will kill you. I told the guys no one is to give you the look while you're testifying. There are to be no threats."

Here it is again, his promise. He's giving me a last gift by making certain I know I'll be safe. From him.

"This is going to be our last conversation, isn't it?" I say, sudden tears filling my eyes.

"I guess so," he replies. "You'll always be in my heart and you'll always be my friend."

I'm crying as I hang up. Whatever else he is or has done, Terry Kelton has been a true friend to me. As badly as I need to escape him, I now know that I'm also going to miss him.

The trial is huge. We're the FBI's star witnesses, just as Jerry promised. They put us up at the Alameda on the Plaza and the U.S. Marshals are at our sides the whole time. They say they're protecting us from Terry's organization, but in reality the only thing we're worried about are the reporters. They're everywhere.

I'm on the stand for only thirty minutes. During my testimony the only man I have to point to is Terry's bodyguard.

That evening back in our hotel room, Steve complains about the ten thousand dollar check we have to write to our lawyer.

I'm floored. After all, I did my job. I kept us out of prison, out of the Witness Protection program and from being killed. And now he doesn't want to do his job?

"This is such a small price to pay for our freedom and our continued lives," I tell him. "Don't you get how important this trial is for us? We're finally free of our past."

He still grumbles.

I receive one more letter from Terry. In it he congratulates me on my performance in court. It's clear from the tone of the letter that he holds no hard feelings for what was said and done, even though it means he's in prison for life.

I fold the letter, feeling a new lightness in my soul. Everything's going to be clear sailing for us from this moment on.

# CHAPTER ELEVEN
# THE (GOOD OLD) BOYS CLUB

September, 1991
Paradise Valley, Arizona

Dear New Board Member:

Again, congratulations on your election to our Board of
Directors. The enclosed new Board member orientation
packet has been designed to offer you as thorough a
background as possible concerning your new organization.

You will find the enclosed literature very helpful.
Included are: a mission statement, an organizational
chart, Board nominating procedures, fundraising
calendar, a map of our facilities, etc. We highly
encourage you to keep this information available as a
reference.

If I, or our President and Executive Director Rick Miller,
can be of any additional assistance, please contact us.

Sincerely
Ed Sucato
Chairman of the Board

I can't fucking believe it. I'm now a member of the corporate board of the Boys and Girls Club of Metropolitan Phoenix. The organization's been around since 1946 and some of the biggest names in the community have been involved, including the Goldwaters, Del Webb, Ed Robson of Robson Communities among others.

And now me.

And, to think three years ago the only club that wanted me was Club Fed.

Better yet, being a member doesn't require much more of me than attending two meetings a year and either writing checks or raising money, although I do have my eye on the Back-to-School shopping event for the boys and girls the organization serves. I'm good at shopping, especially when it comes to buying shoes.

As for why this organization wants me, there are just two words: Affirmative Action. The club needs a woman on their board to keep their United Way funding, which is worth about a million dollars a year to them.

Apparently there'd been a woman member the previous year but she quit after just a few meetings.

That's when Karen Sinchak, our new trust attorney who also does Pro Bono work for the organization, approached us. We hired Karen last year after Steve's trust finally opened, giving us access to all his millions. We have a new trust, one in both our names, called Marigot, after the capital city on the island of Saint-Martin's in the Caribbean, which we discovered and fell in love with on a recent vacation.

Karen thought I'd be perfect for the position because, as she put it, "if you can be friends with that drug dealer guy—you know, the killer?—you can handle these men."

I admit it. I was a little taken aback when she said that. Not that Karen would know about Terry Kelton. I told her about him. I'm still using Amity's three principles to maintain my sober life.

But what the fuck is up with this group of rich old men

that Karen thinks the only woman who can tolerate them is the former best friend of a cold-blooded, psychopathic drug kingpin?

I'll know soon enough. I leave Steve's and my new bedroom dressed in a lightweight gray tweed suit with a red tank top under it. I chose the tweed because it's conservative and the red top because I don't want to appear too staid. I'm wearing flats instead of a higher heel, even though I'm five foot nothing. I don't have to impress anyone tonight. They need me.

In the kitchen I grab my new member packet from the table. Steve grins up at me from his chair. He's going over today's *Wall Street Journal*. Steve loves the stock market. To him, investing in stocks has the same attraction as going to Vegas and laying money on the tables. He usually reads the paper first thing in the morning, but these days it's too noisy. That's because we're living in chaos as we remodel our new home.

Last April out of the blue, Steve asked my real estate agent friend Libby Beckwith to take us house shopping. I figured it was a lark, a chance for us to look into other people's windows and see how the rest of the rich live.

It wasn't. Within four hours Steve had bought a fifty-two hundred square foot Santa Barbara-style fixer-upper with a great view of Camelback, Phoenix's iconic mountain. The massive rusty-red pile of rock really does look like a kneeling camel.

This is the first house we've financed on our own. Our prior home loans were held by the Ralph Sarli National Bank and Trust Company. It's a great outfit, very easy to deal with, but Steve's still trying to put more distance between him and Ralph. So, this time we chose our own bank even though it meant days of Steve struggling through the forms, his Dyslexia making every sentence a chore to read. My favorite moment was when Steve raged for a full half an hour over how wrong it was that a bank could demand to know where and how we make our money.

As for this new house, we're not really living here. We're camping out in a forest made from drywall dust, plastic sheeting and blue tape. This is going to be one long camping trip. According to Carol Minchew, our decorator, we have another six months to go.

The remodel has been great for Steve because he has lots of opportunities to do his job in our marriage: writing checks. I was feeling a little lost now that there are no more drug dealers to run down until Steve put me to work buying all new furniture and artwork for our house.

He doesn't want a home, he wants a showplace. Carol's taken me under her wing, escorting me to galleries and studios across the country, introducing me to artists, craftsmen and gallery owners. She says I'm even beginning to develop a style of my own.

"You look good, Mrs. Corporate Board member," Steve tells me, folding his paper.

"Thanks," I reply. "How are you feeling today?"

There are dark circles under Steve's eyes again. He's been complaining of being tired a lot lately, but every time I suggest he see a doctor he waves away the idea. Men!

"Great," he replies, coming to his feet to pull me close and plant a kiss on my forehead. I give him one in return. It's a habit we've developed. Neither of us ever leaves the house without kissing the other.

Being in a sober relationship has turned out to be much harder than we expected, but Steve and I have a new therapist to see us through the rough patches. Dr. Al Silberman is a Family of Origin specialist, which means he works with the childhood issues that have shaped our adult behavior. Between Steve and me, I think we've given Dr. Al enough material for a couple new books.

"Go get 'em, Mrs. Corporate Board," Steve tells me, releasing me to sit back down at the table and return to his paper. "Just remember if any of them give you trouble, threaten them with Terry Kelton."

That makes me laugh. Steve always knows just what to say to me, that's how well we know each other. My stomach settles and I make my way through a corridor of plastic sheeting until I find our front door.

Although it took me a while, I'm finally in love with this house. This will be my first ever clean house. No one has ever used drugs in this house and no one ever will. It's the house where Steve and I will live out the rest of our clean lives, no matter what I have to do or how hard I need to work to see that it happens.

I drive down our street past the other gorgeous homes and wave at a few people. I don't know why I thought the neighbors here wouldn't be friendly or tap on our door to introduce themselves. I'm already great friends with Dick and Lilli Moss, who live across the street from us. I think I'll adopt Lilli as my second surrogate mother. My decorator Carol is my first.

In just a few minutes I'm taking the turn on Twenty-Fourth Street into the parking lot of the Del E. Webb Administrative Center for the Boys and Girls Club of Metropolitan Phoenix. I made this drive a couple of times earlier this week just to be sure I knew where I was going. According to my new member paperwork, this building houses both a dedicated board room and the charity's administrative offices.

It's a strange looking building. Constructed of cement blocks painted white, it's L-shaped with the long back of the "L" facing Twenty-Fourth Street. I'm sure the architect angled it on its lot this way so there'd be room for the substantial parking lot, but the result is the front of the building doesn't seem to face any of the three streets surrounding it.

With my packet under my arm, I make my way to the building's glass doors. Sweat instantly starts to trickle down the middle of my back. In other places around the world September means the beginning of autumn and cooler temperatures. Not here. It's still over a hundred degrees at sunset.

Inside, I follow the echoing noise of male conversation down a hallway to what must be the dedicated board room and pause in the open doorway. There are about thirty men inside, some standing in chatty clutches, others sitting at the room's ten or so small, round tables. All of them are White and all of them hold drink glasses in their hands. They appear to range in age from thirty-five to seventy, maybe even older.

It's not hard to pick out the corporate guys; they're dressed in serious business suits. With ties, some loosened, some not. The retired guys are just as easy to pick out and not just because they're gray haired. They're all dressed in polo shirts and slacks, looking like they stopped off here after playing eighteen holes. Sprinkled among them are a few guys whose attire suggests they might have once worked with their hands before they became successful enough to afford to buy a seat on this board.

I catch the soprano sound of a woman's laugh. It's the cocktail waitress, a pretty bottle blonde, wearing a really short skirt and a shirt unbuttoned far enough to display an impressive cleavage. Expertly balancing her tray on one hand, she grins as she dances away from a massive man sitting at a table. The guy, a suit who's almost as wide as he is tall, makes one more laughing lunge for her from his chair. He misses. Her hips sway as she heads toward my end of the room and the small bar set up near the door.

"Monica!" Ed Sucato leaves the nearest clutch of men to meet me. A balding, stocky Italian man with a big, friendly smile, he's this year's board chairman. He's dressed more casually than most. He's one of the guys who came up to his position by the fruit of his hands; he owns Sucato Masonry. That somehow makes him seem less intimidating.

Ed's glasses can't hide the way his eyes fill with pleasure as he extends his hand to shake mine. He offers me that great smile of his. "You found us. Come on in. The meeting will start in just a few minutes."

He leads me to a table where one of the serious suits sits, a man in his mid-forties with boyish, clean-cut looks and a thatch of dark hair. There's a small stack of paper on the table next to him. The agenda for tonight's meeting.

"You remember Rick Miller, our president," Ed says as the man comes to his feet and extends his hand for me to shake.

"Oh yes. We met at the black tie auction," I reply, smiling and taking his hand. I remember talking to him for a few minutes.

That auction, held last February, is a major fundraiser for this group. Karen took us as her guests. We went, thinking the event would be the same as the events we'd attended in Kansas City, where showy just isn't done.

Okay, maybe the Allied Food Club annual dinner isn't that upscale considering the membership is mostly grocers and local food manufacturers, but we've attended many cocktail parties with Steve's family held in some fabulous mansions and country clubs. None of them were like this shindig.

You'd have thought we were attending a Hollywood premier. The men were all in professionally tailored tuxedos while most of the women wore long beaded gowns. Gemstone earrings danced in their earlobes while multi-carat diamond rings (I assumed they're diamonds) flashed on many a hand.

Fuck me, even the little sequined evening bags these women carried reflected more light than all the jewelry I wore, which was all my jewelry.

Right now all I own is my wedding set, a solitaire ruby engagement ring and gold wedding band, the Amethyst birthstone ring Steve bought for me and my new diamond tennis bracelet. Steve got it for me off the Home Shopping Network. He loves that show.

"Good to see you again, Monica," Rick says.

"This organization couldn't run without Rick," Ed tells

me. "He does all the heavy lifting. That's why we pay him the big bucks," he finishes with a laugh, giving Rick a clap on the shoulder.

"Right," Rick says with a wry grin then his smile fades into something more serious. "I can't tell you how glad I am you're here, Monica. I could almost say you're saving the life of our organization. Thanks again for considering joining us. Trust me, the satisfaction of helping our kids will make it all worthwhile for you."

I give a shrug to deflect his gratitude. "I'm really looking forward to participating."

The butterflies are back. I'm a little freaked about being on the cutting edge of Affirmative Action. Who would have thought? I wasn't ever into Women's Lib and I never once considered burning my bra. I couldn't. I need that sucker.

"I hope you're still this excited about us after the meeting." Rick crosses his arms and glances to one side. It's that big guy, the one who was flirting with the waitress, he's looking at.

"Some of these guys are a little reluctant about having a woman on the board. I had to tell them that if they didn't want to change all they had to do was raise the million a year the United Way gives us. Everyone knows that's not possible. Although a few of them can be a little outspoken and rough around the edges, there's not one of them who wouldn't move heaven and earth to make life better for the kids we serve."

Rick completely believes what he's just told me. I can see it in his face. Not only is he dedicated to helping Phoenix's kids, he's one hundred percent certain that every member of the corporate board is as well.

My jitters calm as Rick's comment sends me back to the basement of Red's drug house the day a pair of kids no older than eight came looking for their mother, a streetwalker. Red refused to let them go downstairs. He didn't want them seeing their prostitute-mama shooting up. He kept them by the door until she was ready to leave. I'll never forget them peering down the steps at us, looking skinny, dirty, and, I'm sure, hungry.

All of a sudden I know why I'm here. I owe it to those kids to help other kids like them. If what Rick says is true, that at their hearts these guys are all about kids, it says something important about them.

The corner of Rick's mouth twitches. His arms open. "Of course, it helps that it isn't going to be easy to turn your last name into a blue joke the way they did the last woman's." Rick grins, suddenly looking charming, even impish.

It takes me an instant to get it. He's talking about the last woman board member, the one who quit. It rhymed with semen.

Fucking morons.

Laughing, I shake my head. "I was wondering why she left."

Karen was so right about me for this board. I haven't been Ralph's and Steve's Cleaner for more than twenty years without developing a pretty thick skin. Terry and my stint at Amity only toughened it.

I glance around the room again and catch one of the older members giving the cocktail waitress a pat on her butt. There's nothing scary about these guys. They're just a bunch of paunchy old men behaving badly for the one night they're out of sight of their wives.

No wonder they don't want a woman joining them. They don't want to have to behave themselves in their own little clubhouse. I wonder how many of them are shaking in their boots, worried that I might someday tattle on them to their womenfolk.

As I take my place at the table, Rick hands me an agenda. "Time for me to earn those big bucks Ed says they pay me." He moves off, winding his way steadily toward the head of the room.

Ed signals for the cocktail waitress. "What would you

like to drink?" he asks me as she hurries over.

"A soda would be great," I say.

Ed orders his drink and mine as Rick calls the meeting to order. The minutes are read then it's time for the introduction of new members. I'm not the only one, just the only woman.

At last it's my turn to go up front. As I start toward Rick I hear audible groans rise from all around me. Chairs squeak as men shift to stare at me. I glance at the faces around me, expecting hostility. Instead what I see in most of their gazes is resignation. It's more oh shit, I guess I'll have to tolerate her than get the fuck out of here.

That is, all except for that big man. Our gazes meet. He sneers at me. He intends his look to intimidate. I stare back, willing him to bring it on. It's going to take a whole lot more than his rude behavior to drive me off. I've got kids' lives to change.

At the head of the room, I smile and launch into my introduction, wondering what sort of reaction it'll get.

"Hi, I'm Monica Sarli. I first want to say how honored I am to be accepted as a member of the corporate board of the Boys and Girls Club of Metropolitan Phoenix. I'm married to Steve Sarli. He and I are originally from Kansas City, Missouri, but we've lived in the Valley of the Sun for about six years now. Steve is president of his own real estate development firm, Emerald Coast Financial. We're also recovering alcoholics and Heroin addicts. We used for nineteen years before finally cleaning up in 1986. We're very excited to now have the chance to make a difference in our community by working with your organization."

Naya and Bette would be so proud. I glance around the board room. There's not a sound as the men, all except Ed and Rick who already know my story through Karen, stare at me. I've shocked them, even though that wasn't my intention. I just want them to know right up front why I'll always order soda when they offer to buy me a drink. That's just not the sort of libation guys who do business over happy hour or the three martini lunch find easy to accept.

"Come on now, little lady. Are you sure you don't want a shot of vodka to go with your soda?" calls the big guy, breaking the silence.

Although most of the men ignore his comment, enough of them laugh to suggest this fucker has a following in the group. I laugh with them, denying him the reaction he wants then reclaim my seat. The evening continues with committee reports and other such club business. I listen, interested in what they do and where I'll fit in.

By the time Rick closes the meeting an hour or so later, the smell of roast beef is wafting through the air. The caterers have arrived. Before long, waiters are setting plates of prime rib in front of each one of us. The cocktail waitress and bartender get busy refreshing everyone's drinks.

Rick returns to sit at our table for the meal. His voice lowered, he congratulates me on my introduction. I guess he hadn't expected me to be so forthright.

The meal is delicious, far better than I expect. As the waiters clear away the plates, I gather my things, thinking it's time to leave. No one else moves. Well, except for that cocktail waitress. She's once again rushing through the room. This time she's not only replenishing the drinks, she's also laying out decks of cards and poker chips.

So that's why there are so many small tables in the room instead of a few big ones. It's time for poker.

I grin to myself. Bad little boys out on the town, drinking, flirting and playing poker.

I don't even consider leaving. This is perfect. There's no better way to get to know these guys or let them get to know me than over a losing poker hand.

And they will be losing hands, every single one. I'll see to it.

It works. By the end of the evening I've learned that for every asshole like my heckler there are two who applaud my sobriety. As often happens when I run my story, a few men even confide in me about their own struggles with addiction. And, for every one of the guys who suggests it's fine if I want to stay away from these boring old meetings and be a member in name only, there are men like Jack Gleason.

Jack is a vice president at the Del Webb Corporation and originally from the Los Angeles area. He's short but good looking and he carries himself the way Ralph does, like a man accustomed to giving orders and having them obeyed. Unlike Ralph, there's something more about him, something inviting and personable, so much so that I instantly decide to volunteer for the black tie auction organizing committee because it's the one Jack's wife works on.

As we talk, I'm excited to learn that he and his wife Betty also live in Clearwater Hills, on the block behind my house. He tells me that he's determined to give this board a more professional image. I think that translates to: I want fewer good old boys who heckle a woman because she has a suggestive last name and more members, male or female, who understand good public relations.

By the time the poker games finally wrap up and we're all leaving, I'm smiling and waving to the guys I've put on my list of future friends for Steve and me: Ed, Jack, Larry Cummings, Mal Straus, Jim Schlesing, Frank Brady. All of them are successful professionals and not one is a user. I can't wait to meet their wives, or for these guys to meet Steve.

That's when I realize I've completely reclaimed my old job. I'm once more managing Steve's and my relationships, only this time they're sober, positive relationships. In the next months I'll be building friendships with these new men and their wives, creating a new healthy circle for me and Steve.

I can't wait to step into our future, one where Steve uses his money to make a difference for the kids of Phoenix while I entertain our new friends. That's when I give thanks for the two women in my life whose training makes my transition from user to socialite possible.

Not Bette and Naya this time, but my mother and Mary Helen.

Both my mother and Mary Helen were raised in upper middle class households where proper social etiquette was just how things were done. My grandfather Joseph Tedrow, an army buddy of Harry Truman's, was a highly successful Kansas City lawman. He once chased Bonnie and Clyde and there's now a section of the University of Missouri Kansas City law library named for him. Grandfather married Martha Payne Tedrow after my grandmother, Mom's mother, passed away when Mom was twelve.

Martha, the only one of my grandparents who survived long enough for me to know, was an unattractive but well-to-do and social climbing farm girl from Fayette, Missouri, who, by the time I knew her was living in an elegant apartment with Bill, another woman.

It's amazing how much you can insinuate in a single sentence. Now, I don't know if Martha really was a lesbian or just bi. Or neither of those. After all she and Bill, whose real name was Mildred, slept in separate rooms; Martha used the apartment's rear bedroom while Bill slept in the front one. Bill needed the larger room because of her furniture. She had a beautiful bedroom set, including a four poster canopy bed I coveted. Bill also needed the closet space. She kept her vodka bottles in her closet, both full and empty.

Stacks and stacks of bottles. But that was Bill, not Martha.

Guided by Martha's earlier training and ambitions, Mom saw to it that my sister and I mastered the social graces. We learned how to set a table, including where to put the coffee cup and what a fish fork is, and how to write proper thank you notes, required for any gift given or good deed done me. When I was young the social graces also included wearing little white gloves and black patent leather Mary Janes when the four of us went shopping downtown, something I'm grateful I no longer have to do.

Gloves aside, Mom's foundation left me properly prepared for joining Mary Helen in the country club lifestyle that Martha had so longed for. It was Mary Helen who taught me to be comfortable in any social situation, including what to wear when, and how to carry on a polite conversation.

As I think of Mary Helen, I smile again. Once I've got me and Steve established in this new circle of ours, I'm going to have a party and introduce our new friends to my in-laws. That will be the day Ralph tells me and Steve how proud he is of us.

Nothing can stop us now.

# CHAPTER TWELVE
# WE ROLL A SEVEN

*May, 1992*
*The home of Barry Goldwater*
*Paradise Valley, Arizona*

I cannot believe it. This little Republican girl is standing on Barry Goldwater's fabulous patio enjoying his amazing view of central Phoenix.

That's right, the Barry Goldwater. Longtime Arizona senator. Former presidential candidate. Statesman. General all around world class celebrity.

A chili dinner for ten couples, the chili cooked by Barry himself, was an auction item at last February's Boys and Girls Club black tie event, the first one I helped coordinate. I wanted to be part of this event more than I wanted to breathe. So, Steve and I recruited the five couples we now proudly claim as our friends, the Gleasons, the Cummings, the Bradys, the Schlesings and the Nadlers, set our price limit and elected Steve as our designated bidder. The action was fast and furious, but Steve came out victorious. All that was left to do was find three more couples to fill out the evening, which we did easily.

Now here I am, on Barry's flagstone patio this balmy seventy degree evening watching the overcast sky turn pink, then orange, then purple. It's another fantastic Arizona sunset. Behind me, conversations ebb and flow, spiked with laughter and the scrape of chairs being pulled across the stones. Glasses clink as drinks are refilled. Dinner's almost ready. I can smell the chili cooking.

Twilight deepens to midnight blue. A bat darts drunkenly across the sky, chasing some insect I can't see. The streetlights in the valley below me burst to life and ordinary asphalt roads become twinkling sequined bands.

That's how my life feels right now, all dressed up in sparkle and flash. I have arrived and satisfaction is as powerful as any drug I've ever used.

I'm just about ready to turn and find my table, when Brad Burgess comes to stand next to me. Brad's the B in CBS Realty, a local commercial real estate firm; our friend Jim Schlesing is the S.

"Monica, I think I'm glad Jim couldn't make it tonight and asked me to pinch hit for him," Brad says.

I smile at Brad. I like both him and his wife Jo, but I'm sorry Jim and Beth aren't here. I enjoy every minute I spend with them because I love the way they treat each other. I'd like to pattern my new sober relationship with Steve after their marriage.

Brad crosses his arms, staring out at the darkening city. "I think what most impresses me is that radio set up of his. I can't wait to see how it works," Brad says, speaking of Barry's ham radio. Barry's promised to fire it up after we eat.

I laugh. "My Grandmother Martha had a ham radio when I was young. I remember talking to people all over the world," I tell Brad. I loved it when Martha would put me in her lap and let me spin the dial.

Behind us the patio door opens. We both turn. Senator Goldwater steps outside. He's bent and frail, but no one would mistake him for anyone but Barry Goldwater. He looks just like his photos, the gray hair, the dark rimmed glasses, although I've never seen a photo of him wearing a Tommy Bahama-type print shirt like he does tonight.

Barry takes a seat at the head table as those of our group remaining in the house begin to trickle outside. Everyone else circles, looking for their names on the place cards. I don't need to look. I know exactly where Steve and I are sitting: right next to the senator and his wife, Susan.

I'm grinning again, my heart skipping happily in my chest. "Looks like it's time to eat," I tell Brad, eager to claim my place of honor among these people.

"You know what I want, Jack?" Steve's loud voice cuts through the evening, catching our attention. He's standing next to our seats at the table, talking to Jack Gleason. They look like Mutt and Jeff standing there, heavyset Steve towering over short, slim Jack. "I want my name on that wall down at the Boys and Girls Club, the one where you have all those plaques. Monica and I love helping the kids, but I want to be remembered. I want to be one of the big contributors. Help me figure out some way to make that happen."

Jack's glasses glint, reflecting the patio lighting as he looks up at Steve. As always Jack looks a little more dressed up than anyone else tonight in his creased chinos and button front shirt. At least the shirt has short sleeves. That's about as casual as he gets.

"Well Steve, the first thing that comes to my mind is a matching pledge drive."

I've seen that look on Jack's face before. I think a shark sensing blood in the water must look about the same, only in this case it's the look of a corporate board member sensing a major donation for the kids.

"What do you think, Frank?" Jack asks, looking at Frank Brady, who, like Jack, has been drawn in by the smell of a future donation.

Frank's tall and fit with dark hair graying at the temples. He's a partner at Ernst and Young and a member of the Paradise Valley Country Club, to which he's sponsored us to join. Carol and Weldon are our co-sponsors. Until our application is finally approved, Steve's happily playing the course as Frank's and Weldon's guest.

"We haven't done one of those in a while," Frank says. "It's about time to send someone new to milk some of the local corporations and money guys for more donations. What'd you think, Steve? We'll help you with the list. Can you pledge ten thousand then get these guys to match your donation with their own?"

From across the patio I watch as Steve glances toward the senator then says even more loudly, "Ten thousand? Is that all I have to give? That's just a drop in the bucket for me."

All my satisfaction with the evening wilts, leaving only embarrassment.

Jack's wife Betty steps close and puts her arm around my shoulders. "Well my dear, I see Steve's in rare form tonight."

I laugh to cover how much Steve's bragging bothers me before I remember that this is Betty. We're good enough friends that she knows exactly how I feel about what Steve does. "Why does he always have to be this way, Betty? It's so obnoxious. I mean, it's not as if anyone here cares how much money he has."

"He's just trying to fit in," Betty assures me, doing what she always does, smoothing out the rough edges. "He means well. Poor guy. He reminds me of a St. Bernard puppy, big, awk-ward, but good at heart. And cute."

As she finishes, she gives me one of her million dollar smiles and instantly everything about her face, from her eyes to the lift of her brows and the curve of her mouth reminds me of her father. I've never met him, but I know who he is: Robert Young, as in Father Knows Best and Marcus Welby, MD.

I'm comforted by the thought of others seeing Steve as

a St. Bernard puppy. And Betty's right. Steve really does mean well.

Then Betty adds, "I will say that Steve's looking a little worn these days."

I forget about puppies in the face of my growing concern over Steve's health. "He does, doesn't he?"

Steve's energy level is so low that he naps all the time. A few weeks back I finally put my foot down and forced him to go to the Mayo Clinic for a checkup. They must have found something because he had to have a liver biopsy. Steve's supposed to get the results next week.

"Time to eat," I say, linking my arm in hers.

I love—love!—our new life.


*June, 1992*
*Mayo Clinic*
*Scottsdale, Arizona*

Steve's half-sitting on the examining table, one foot on the floor, the other jiggling nervously. Since this isn't an exam, he's still in his street clothes. When he sees me looking at him, he makes a face at me, and then combs his fingers through his hair.

Steve always finds it hard to hold still for any length of time, but he's especially jumpy today. That tells me he's really nervous and makes me glad I decided to come with him to this appointment. Steve's Dyslexia makes it hard for him to absorb what he hears, and being nervous makes it worse.

He reaches for my hand and I give his fingers a reassuring squeeze before turning my attention back on the doctor.

Dr. Keats, Mayo Clinic Scottsdale's liver specialist, sits in front of us on a little rolling stool, his head bowed over Steve's file. He's middle aged and fairly good looking, which means in his white coat with his stethoscope draped around his neck he looks like every other Mayo Clinic doctor I've seen.

I swear somewhere in the bowels of this building lurks a secret lab where Mayo manufactures these guys. They're the Stepford doctors of medical profession. Not that they're not great doctors. It's just a little strange how alike they all look.

Paper rustles as he flips the pages. The clock on the wall behind him ticks gently. Through the closed door I can hear the PA system as the nurse makes garbled nonsense of some other patient's name.

He finally closes the file and looks up at us. "You both understand what Hepatitis C is, right?"

"Not really," I reply for both Steve and me.

"Maybe you heard it mentioned as Non-A, Non-B Hepatitis? That's what it would have been called back when Steve contracted it."

I shake my head a little surprised to learn that Steve has contracted a disease either now or in the past. Or maybe not. Steve's done his share of contracting diseases, most of them sexually transmitted, Syphilis and Gonorrhea to name a few. But I've never heard of this Hepatitis C.

"Up until recently Hepatitis C has been a bit of a mystery disease," Dr. Keats informs us. "We finally know that it's contracted much like AIDS, through promiscuous sex, blood transfusions and intravenous drug use. But Steve I see here," he taps the file folder, "that in 1979 you had Hepatitis B when you had your pulmonary abscess. That's most likely when and how you got the Hepatitis C."

I stifle a nervous giggle. What was I thinking? This disease fits right into the class of diseases Steve usually gets, although this time it doesn't seem he got it from putting his dick in the wrong place, something he hasn't done recently, thank God. I glance at Steve to see if he gets the irony, but he's still staring intently at the doctor.

Yes, back in '79, Steve had a pulmonary abscess. And, just as the doctor says, he also had Hepatitis B, as well as

Jaundice and more. He was so sick that he nearly died, and ended up staying in the hospital for weeks. Back then the doctors told us, but not Ralph, that Steve most likely got the pulmonary abscess from his intravenous drug use.

Or more precisely, from shooting up so often and using dirty needles.

"Why didn't anyone mention back then that I had this C?" Steve asks.

I again give his fingers a squeeze. The fact that he asks a question the doctor's just explained tells me he's scared and overwhelmed.

Dr. Keats shakes his head. "Your doctors back then might not have found it. As I said, Hep C wasn't really on our radar until recently. That's why we needed to do the liver biopsy. The biopsy is the only way we can determine how long you've had this disease and how well your liver's coping with it."

He again taps his forefinger against Steve's closed file folder. "The biopsy confirms that you've had the disease for the past thirteen years and you now have what I call a smoldering liver."

"What's a smoldering liver?" I ask.

"It's like a smoldering fire, still smoking but not flaming or out of control," Dr. Keats replies, smiling at his own analogy. "That means we definitely see liver damage, but it's not getting any worse. It's also not getting any better."

I'm still struggling with the idea of Steve having a disease I've never heard of. "But if Steve has this Hepatitis C, why doesn't he feel or act sick? All he's complained of is being tired."

"Good question," Dr. Keats replies almost cheerfully. "It's actually not uncommon for some people to display no symptoms with Hepatitis C. In fact, almost a third of the folks who have it aren't at all inconvenienced by it until they develop Cirrhosis. Among the other two-thirds tiredness is the most common complaint."

He shifts to look directly at Steve. "It's important to note that no matter what symptoms patients display, Hepatitis C is always fatal," he informs Steve gently.

The doctor's words hit me like a blow, driving all the air out of my lungs. Gasping, I turn to look at my husband, clutching his hand to my chest. He stares back at me, his eyes wide. There's no color in his face.

I'm looking at a dead man.

Tears fill my eyes. I won't let Steve die. I can't. I need Steve. He's my everything. Who would I be if I wasn't Mrs. Steve Sarli?

Steve looks back at the doctor. "I'm dying?" he demands, his voice raspy.

I wait for the doctor's answer, every fiber in my being willing him to save Steve for me.

Dr. Keats gives a shake of his head. "Generally speaking. Most people who contract Hep C live for about twenty years after contraction. We're estimating you've had it for thirteen years, Steve. If nothing changes in your general health and overall condition, then I'd say you're on course to develop Cirrhosis in about seven years."

"Seven years," I cry as every muscle in my body weakens with relief. My head spins with it. Seven years isn't dying. Next month is dying, or maybe next year. Seven years, that's time enough to figure out how to fix this. I get to keep my Steve.

I look at the only man I've ever loved. "Did you hear him?"

"I heard," Steve mumbles and pulls his hand from mine.

I'm not ready to release him, not now that I'm sure I get to keep him. But as I reach for him, he fidgets away from me, rubbing his hands over his face as his dangling foot jerks even more rapidly.

Steve doesn't need to say another word. His actions tell me he's upset and overwhelmed, and that for the next little while he'll be lost in himself.

But I'm not. I know exactly where and who I am. I am Mrs. Steve Sarli and Mrs. Steve Sarli's job is to keep her husband alive. That's something she's been successfully doing for years, through overdoses, pistol whippings, murdered friends and Terry Kelton.

Turning to the doctor, I draw myself up to my tallest, my fists tight and my shoulders squared. What I need now is a plan. Better yet, I need Narcaine, like that night at Monk's, Narcaine for Hepatitis C.

"So, what's our next step? What medicines does Steve need to take? What's the treatment plan?" I'm not asking these questions, I'm commanding the answers. The doctor will tell me how to heal Steve.

Dr. Keats eases back on his stool, clasping his hands around one knee as he looks at me. "If he qualifies for inclusion, you should definitely consider adding Steve's name to the liver transplant list. But don't get your hopes up. It's a very long list and there's no guarantee he'll move up fast enough to receive one in time.

In time? I reject his qualifier. We've got plenty of time, a whole seven years' worth.

"Also," the doctor continues, "the costs for a transplant can be upwards of two hundred and fifty thousand dollars. The best thing Steve can do now is concentrate on keeping himself healthy. We encourage our Hep C patients to pay special attention to their diets, avoiding fats and junk food, which tax the liver."

Beside me, Steve makes a lost sound. I glance at him to see that he's again rubbing his face then frowns at the doctor. I'm looking for Narcaine and he's talking impossible liver transplants and watching what Steve eats?

"Seriously? That's it?"

"The healthier Steve and his liver stay, the longer he lives," Dr. Keats assures me. "There's no certainty to the progression of this disease or how quickly Steve's liver may succumb. Diet and regular exercise can potentially add as much as ten years to his life."

I snatch these words out of the air and tuck them into my pocket. Now we're talking. Ten plus seven is seventeen years. For that, I can watch Steve's diet and make sure he goes to the gym.

"Does golf count as exercise?" I ask.

Dr. Keats considers for moment. "I suppose, as long as he's walking the course, not riding in a cart. A gym program would probably be better."

I'm still thinking about how I'll get Steve to the gym when the doctor clears his throat. It's an uncomfortable sound. I glance at him. He watches me intently as he straightens on his stool.

"You need to address your sexual activity. It wouldn't be wise to practice any risqué bedroom behavior. You two aren't into any S and M practices, are you?""

"Sadomasochism?" I blurt out, stunned and gaping.

Dr. Keats makes that uncomfortable sound again. "Yes, it wouldn't be wise to do anything that might result in drawing blood, especially anal sex."

"What are you talking about?" I gasp out. My husband is deathly ill and the doctor wants to talk about anal sex? "Steve and I have been married for sixteen years."

Although Steve and I do have sex, it's not the focus of our relationship. It never has been. It's even less so now that Steve's been too tired to perform.

The doctor offers a nervous smile. "It just needed to be said. And of course, with his liver damage, Steve must absolutely avoid alcohol and drugs," he continues, sounding more comfortable as he leaves behind the subject of sex. "His liver absolutely cannot process alcohol or drugs," the doctor reiterates.

"That's no problem. We're recovering addicts and we're maintaining our sobriety," I say, speaking for both of us and making what has become a rote statement for me. The doctor should know this already, because I know we included the information on our addiction in Steve's medical history.

Dr. Keats' brows rise in surprise. "Is that so? Well, then Steve definitely qualifies for addition to the transplant list. Hmm," he says, again bowing his head over Steve's file as he flips to a page and reads. This time the only sounds in the room are the tick of the clock and Steve repeated heavy sighs. Sighing is another indication that Steve's frightened.

The doctor looks up after a moment. "As long as he doesn't drink or drug, I think Steve might be a good candidate for Interferon treatments."

I want to shout with joy. I knew there'd be a Narcaine for Hepatitis C! I want to dance. I want to grab Steve's hands and make him dance with me.

"Don't get too excited," Dr. Keats says, holding up a cautioning hand. "At best Interferon is only a stopgap. It might slow Steve's liver deterioration, if Steve happens to fall into the lucky sixty percent of people for whom Interferon works. But, if it does work, it could potentially add yet another ten years to his life."

That's all it takes. I'm instantly certain Steve's in the lucky percentile. Of course he is. Haven't we always been in that group? Look at how we survived Terry Kelton and the FBI. There's no reason for it to be any different now.

One more time I do the math. Seven plus ten for healthy eating plus maybe another ten with the Interferon adds up to twenty-seven years. Steve's already forty. That's means he'll live to be sixty seven. And who knows? By that time they may have a cure for this disease.

I nudge Steve with my elbow as the doctor starts explaining how Interferon works. He needs to pay attention to this. Although Steve stops sighing and turns his gaze on Dr. Keats, there's no way to be sure he's actually listening.

"You'll be injecting yourself every other day. There are some side effects," Dr. Keats warns. "You might even feel more tired than you do now. The Interferon is very delicate, requiring constant refrigeration, and it's not inexpensive, running about seven-hundred and fifty dollars a month. If you'd like we can start you on the program as early as next week," he concludes.

I'm about to say go, but before I can speak Steve comes to his feet. He looks like he's ready to run from the room. "Do I have to start the treatment right away?"

I stare at him in surprise. What does he fucking mean, does he have to? Of course he does. This is his rescue plan.

"Is there a problem?" Dr. Keats asks, glancing from Steve to me, a reminder that it's my job to see to it Steve lives.

"We're going on an European cruise in August," Steve says. "It doesn't sound like this Interferon stuff will travel well."

"We should cancel the trip, hon," I suggest, wanting to reach out and shake him.

"No, I want to go," Steve replies sharply. "We've been looking forward to this trip for a while and from what Dr. Keats says it sounds like we won't be traveling for the year I have to take this stuff."

I blink in surprise. Oh. He was listening. Well, that's good, except all I can think of is that EMT telling me the sooner the Narcaine got into Steve's system, the sooner the danger was gone.

"Realistically, a few months delay isn't going to make a critical difference," the doctor seconds, adding his vote for Steve. "But you shouldn't delay any more than that."

I consider arguing, but the set of Steve's jaw tells me it would be a waste of time.

With that, our interview is over. After scheduling Steve for a few more tests, we make our way out of the Clinic. Steve walks with his head lowered as if watching his feet.

I wait until we're in the car before I ask, "How are you doing, babe?"

"How do you think I'm doing?" Steve retorts, shoving the key into the ignition without looking at me. "I'm dying."

"You are not," I snap back. "The doctor said nothing's really certain about what's happening to you. If you follow his orders, keep yourself healthy and do the Interferon for sure you'll have another twenty years. You have to think positive. We can beat this."

Steve slams his hand on the steering wheel, then wrenches around in the seat to glare at me. "You weren't listening," he shouts. "He said I'm dying and they can't do anything to stop it."

The anger crumples out of his face. For an instant, his blue eyes are wide and filled with fear then it's like the shutters closing. All the emotion disappears from his gaze.

"And, you know what?" he informs me as calmly as if we were discussing where to go for dinner. "If I'm dying, then I'm going to do whatever the hell I want to until I go."

I stare at him, stunned. Not by the part about Steve doing whatever he pleases. Steve always does exactly what he wants. As he should.

That's what my mother and Mary Helen taught me. The man in the relationship gets to do what he wants while the woman waits to see what's left over for her. That's how I've been operating for so long I don't even recognize I'm doing it any more.

Instead, it's his words *I'm dying* that has me tongue-tied. I hear it in Steve's voice. He absolutely believes it. I stare at him, feeling Steve slip away from me.

I won't let it happen. From this moment on, I will be strong for both of us. I worked too hard to get us here, I won't be defeated now.

He tears his gaze from mine then jams the car into reverse.

# CHAPTER THIRTEEN
## STILL HOLDING ON

*October, 1992*
*Paradise Valley, Arizona*

I'm in my upstairs dining room with Weldon, Carol Minchew's husband and my contractor. Weldon's actually a guest at my party today, but I figured since he was here I'd show him a few more items I think his crew should fix. Poor Weldon. The first time he told me to go through the house with blue tape and mark the things that either weren't done right or weren't finished he came back to walls almost completely covered with tape.

After almost a year, six months longer than his decorator-wife Carol's prediction, our remodel is nearing the finish line. Steve's fixer-upper has been transformed from down-at-the-heels Santa Barbara to gorgeous Tuscan villa. The color scheme is timeless: old bronze, silver, gold, taupe, charcoal and smoky brown. The powerful artwork I spent a year collecting makes every room something special.

Our house is so beautiful we've been asked to participate in this year's ASID's Tour de Noel, an annual local home tour that raises money for charity. There are magazines interested in writing feature articles about it.

But not until I say the work is finished. Hey, considering what Steve's paying Weldon, I think every inch of the house should be perfect. I'm lucky he and Carol love me, because I'm a serious pain in the ass.

"Hey Monica, we need you outside," calls Sue Cummings from downstairs with the rest of my guests. Actually, most of the guests aren't in the house, they're out on the patio. It's a beautiful day, with a bright blue cloudless sky and the temperature a cool ninety degrees.

That's right, I used the words cool and ninety degrees in the same sentence. Beginning at the end of September those of us who live in the Phoenix area, even here in Paradise Valley, start holding our breaths, waiting, praying, for daytime temperatures to finally drop below one hundred degrees. Of course when it does we all immediately break out our down jackets because for us seventy degrees is cold.

So, today the French doors in my house's downstairs entry are open so guests can flow in and out.

"What for?" I call down to Sue.

"Larry and Steve are going to do the Jackie Gleason thing," she tells me.

"Be right there. Don't let them start without me."

"Will do," Sue calls back.

"What's the Jackie Gleason thing?" Weldon asks. Weldon looks like exactly what he is: a good old boy from Texas. He's got the sun beaten face and the rough hands, everything but the cowboy boots. He's more of a polo shirt and golf shoe sort of guy. Weldon knows Larry, who is one of my fellow board members, because he and Carol are often my guests at Boys and Girls Club events.

"Steve and Larry were goofing off the other day, just being silly. You know how Steve can be," I add, still clinging to that Saint Bernard puppy image of Betty's. "Before long they had come up with the Ralph and Larry Kramden Show."

"Like *The Honeymooners*? I can see Steve in Jackie

Gleason's Ralph role. He's even starting to look like him," Weldon says with a smile. It's a reminder that Weldon really likes Steve. Most people do, accepting him despite his sometimes blowhard ways. "But why the Ralph and Larry show?"

"Because there is no Ed Norton," I reply, referring to Art Carney's character in the show, "only Ralphs. And, it's the Ralph and Larry Show because Ralph is Steve's first name." Steve's full name is Ralph Stephen Sarli.

"This I gotta see," Weldon says, putting his note into his pocket and following me down the stairs.

As we descend into my house's lower entryway we cross the doorway to my Media room. It's a comfortable space with cream colored walls and a built-in entertainment center filling one wall. The furnishings include a McGuire table and matching chairs, an octagon shaped coffee table carved from a solid piece of Travertine and a leather sectional.

That's where Ralph Sarli sits, at one end of the sectional. He's talking with our own local Jack Gleason, who stands in front of him, and Dick Moss, my neighbor, who sits beside him. Dick's a former Kansas Citian, who was a vice president at Southwest Bell before he retired. He still looks the part of successful executive with his conservatively cut white hair and his preppy attire.

This is it. The party I've been planning for over a year now, the one where I introduce Ralph and Mary Helen to our new friends and they put their stamp of approval on Steve's and my new, clean and sober lives.

Actually, Steve's parents aren't specifically in town to see us. They came for the USC-ASU football game. Ralph's an alum of the University of Southern California, and a die-hard football fan. They rarely miss a game, away or home.

Given a choice Ralph would have turned his back on American Beauty and stayed in LA after he completed his degree. Hollywood had caught his eye. He'd even earned a little money as an extra in a number of movies. But, Mama Nicolena wasn't having any of that from Rocco's only male heir. She commanded Ralph to return to Kansas City. Ralph said he cried all the way home.

Today, my father-in-law looks as happy as I've ever seen him. His eyes sparkle almost as brightly as the cut glass drink tumbler he holds in his hand. He's in his element, holding forth with other captains of industry.

He catches sight of me and smiles. I offer a wiggle of my fingers as Weldon and I make our way through the open doors and onto the flagstone patio. Artfully placed boulders and big pots are set around the tiled pool. Our mature trees and tall palms offer inviting islands of shade. Bougainvilleas, planted by a previous owner, climb the side of the house and wind through the wrought iron railing at the edge of the second story balcony. Their vibrant red blossoms and glossy green foliage suggest Italy.

Sue Cummings is waiting for me just outside the door, standing with Mary Helen. They're both tall, slim, blonde—well, Mary Helen's hair color is more frosted than blonde—and elegant. Looking smart in her pantsuit, Mary Helen's makeup is flawless and every hair is in place. Sue, fashion model pretty, wears a flowing skirt and strappy top, although she'd look elegant in a gunny sack. Her makeup is flawless and her hair is beautifully arranged.

They both offer me easy, generous smiles, and I'm taken aback by how alike they look in that instant. Like Ralph, Mary Helen is also in her element. It's only when I see my mother-in-law like this that I remember she was as good a catch for Ralph as he was for her.

"Here you are," Sue says to me, taking my arm. "Come and watch, Mary Helen. You too, Weldon," she invites.

Weldon and Mary Helen, her tumbler cradled close to her chest, follow Sue and me as we cross to the closer of the two cabanas in my backyard. This horseshoe-shaped open-air structure has stucco walls and a beehive fireplace. It's big enough to hold a Limestone patio table and six chairs.

Right now, the table is pushed to one side and those of

my guests not inside are using the rearranged chairs. Waiting for us at the forefront of the cabana are Steve and Larry.

Sue's husband and Steve are the perfect men to stage this little skit. Although they're both more fair-haired than Ralph Kramden, they do look a lot like a middle aged Jackie Gleason, being tall, barrel-chested men just beginning to show a bit of jowl. But, it's their big shot, loudmouthed mannerisms that make them Ralph Kramdens.

"Show's about to start, folks," Larry announces.

Larry is CEO of The Cummings Group, his own advertising agency and Sue's fourth husband. Or is it fifth? What does it matter? Sue's got a great guy this time.

"We're ready," Sue tells Larry as we join Betty, Dick's wife Lilli, Carol, and my next door neighbors the Malones, at one side of the cabana.

Larry looks at Steve. Steve's grinning from ear to ear, completely enjoying himself at center stage. They nod, then as one, they ball up their fists and say, "To the moon, Alice."

Everyone laughs, even Mary Helen. Steve and Larry follow this with other lines from *The Honeymooners*: *One of these days, Alice, one of these days* and *har har hardee har har*.

We make them repeat it when Ralph, Jack and Dick join us, then everyone drifts back to eating and drinking.

A little while later I'm in the downstairs kitchen checking the appetizer tray when I hear Steve talking. His voice is suddenly booming, a sure sign he's about to show off.

"I told Weldon and Carol that I wanted a showplace and that's what they gave me. I told them to spare no expense," he says.

"And we didn't," Weldon shoots back, laughing.

I step into the kitchen doorway. Weldon and Steve are standing in front of our big screen TV. Ralph's again on the sectional, sharing the sofa with Betty and Jack now. They're all watching Steve as he talks to our neighbors, the Malones.

Weldon puts his arm around Steve's shoulders. "Just remember, Steve. You're my annuity. You just keep paying and paying." He winks.

Steve laughs. "That's right. Four hundred thousand and counting."

The party breaks up an hour or so later. Leaving Mary Helen downstairs, Ralph joins Steve and me as we bid every-one goodbye. Steve leaves to escort the last of the guests outside, and Ralph looks at me. Every cell of his face radi-ates pride.

"Very nice party and very nice people," he tells me in approval. Then he laughs. "Yep, great party, great house. Must be nice to be able to afford a house like this. I don't live in a house this nice."

I laugh. Ralph's kidding. I think. Ralph's never been a keep-up-with-the-Joneses sort of guy.

"Well, that's your choice, isn't it?" I retort. "You could af-ford any house you want. I think you're just cheap, Ralph."

Ralph sends me a sidelong look. "I built that house of ours just before Steve was born and I'm never leaving it. Mary Helen will have to drag me out of it."

Now, this I believe. Because I think we're getting too serious I offer Ralph the first line of what has become our traditional joke over the years. "Just remember, you can't take it with you."

He grins and dutifully supplies the other half. "Well if I can't take it with, then I'm not going."

Then we both remember we're joking about death and we fall silent. Ralph's face softens. "How's Steve really do-ing?" he asks.

I reluctantly step back into my real life. "I make sure he follows Dr. Keats' instructions, and watch his diet and keep him exercising. We walk every day. And he's taking the In-terferon. All we can do is pray and hope for the best."

Ralph releases a long, slow breath. "That's good. I know I can count on you to keep him on the straight and narrow."

And here we are again, me once more Ralph's Cleaner, the person Ralph counts on to take care of Steve so Ralph doesn't have to worry. So Ralph can go back and live his normal life while I live with Steve.

I wish my life were normal. These days I feel like I'm dogpaddling in a flood. I even started having panic attacks again. I haven't had one since the first days of my friendship with Terry Kelton.

Like they always have, the attack came out of the blue. I went to step on an escalator and all of a sudden my head was spinning and my heart started pounding like it wanted to jump out of my chest. Sweat soaked me. I had to back away from the stairs and sit down until it passed.

Ralph and I are still watching the door, waiting for Steve to return, when Mary Helen climbs the stairs and joins us. She yet holds her tumbler, newly refilled to the brim with amber liquid.

"Monica, that was a lovely cocktail party," Mary Helen says. "Your friends are all great. What a fun group. That Sue Cummings, now there's a great gal. She's really lovely. She and her husband make a great couple."

"He's a card, that one," Ralph chuckles, talking about Larry. "What a sense of humor. You should encourage Steve to spend all his time with Larry."

At the mention of Steve, Mary Helen goes from smiling socialite to disapproving mother. "What's going on with Steve?" she demands. "All he does is talk about money and how much he's spending. You'd think he'd hit the lottery the way he's thrown money at this house."

She's as conservative as Ralph when it comes to their wealth. Well, when it comes to spending their money on themselves, anyway. When it comes to their kids, they spare no expense. Steve got a brand new Chevelle for his sixteenth birthday. When he totaled it a week later, Ralph bought him another new car.

I wholeheartedly agree with Mary Helen. Even though I love my house and wouldn't have it any other way, the amount of cash that slips through Steve's fingers these days concerns me, too.

"Yeah, winning the lottery." Ralph nods at Mary Helen as if thanking her for better describing his concern about Steve. "That's exactly how it sounded to me too with all that talk about how much he spent on this or that."

Ralph then looks at me and his eyes narrow in warning. "You know, it looks like you've got a big problem here with that." His usually gruff voice deepens in command and I'm once again Ralph's loyal manager while he's CEO of the Steve endeavor. "You need to do something about it, quick."

"What are you going to do about it?" Mary Helen asks.

I look at them and am suddenly crushed under the weight of their expectations when I was expecting praise and acceptance. What the fuck do they expect me to do, chain Steve to the wrought iron balcony?

"Steve's a grown up. It's his money," I say, throwing my hands wide in frustration. "If I try to say anything about what he's doing, he explodes at me."

That isn't the response Ralph expects from his Cleaner. He grunts. "Well, I don't know how you're going to fix it. I just know you need to fix it."

Mary Helen nods in agreement as she lifts her glass to her lips.

I glance between them. All their earlier pride is gone as if it never existed. Just like that, we're back in the hospital room after Steve's overdose, with them loving Steve, wanting to be proud of him, but utterly certain he's only going to screw up again and ruin everything. And that's more than they can tolerate.

# CHAPTER FOURTEEN
## YOU NEVER LET ME DO WHAT I WANT

*September 1993*
*Malee's on Main*
*Scottsdale, Arizona*

"You're looking a little tired, Monica," Carol says, sipping her tea. Malee's is one of my favorite restaurants. I love the lush ambience, all golden walls and red silk chairs, and the food's great, too.

Carol looks fabulous as always. To me, she epitomizes casual elegance with her artsy jewelry and her fondness for loose, flowing attire. Her hair, prematurely white, is always styled in the newest contemporary cut. "Is everything okay? The Valley Fever isn't back, is it?"

There are only three drawbacks to living in the Phoenix area, better known to those of us who live here as the Valley of the Sun: excessive heat (and sunshine), dust storms, and Valley Fever, a nasty little lung infection caused by a fungus that lives in Phoenix's soil. Most cases consist of mild, Flu-like symptoms. Not mine. At its worst I was so tired I could barely walk up and down my stairs.

"I don't think so," I sigh. "I think I'm just overwhelmed.

Not only am I planning next year's auction for the Boys and Girls Club, I also agreed to co-chair next year's Cancer Gala." I wouldn't have done it except I really like my co-chairs.

Oh fuck, I can't lie. I was seduced by the thought of arranging one of the most prestigious charity balls on Phoenix's social calendar.

Charity balls. They're Prom on steroids. There's a theme, and a decorated room, a hotel ballroom not a gymnasium. And no crepe paper. Instead, it's all gorgeous flower arrangements, beautiful tablecloths, careful lighting and live music courtesy of some well-known local band that can play everything from standards to rock.

Although there's no king and queen, there's definitely royalty in the room, in this case the honorary chairs. Recruited by the organizers, their only real function is to write a very large check to the cause.

"I guess I didn't realize how much handshaking, corporate-office-visiting and dignified pleading for donations I'd have to do to get the Gala off the ground," I add with a smile, and Carol laughs.

With that, I plow into more personal matters. "Oh, Carol. Nothing's been right between Steve and me since he started the Interferon." Carol and Weldon have both known about Steve's Hep C since the day we got the diagnosis. I doubt we could have kept it from them; we were practically living together during the remodel. "That restaurant only makes it worse."

A while back Steve formed a partnership with some friends and bought a restaurant. It's been a money pit from the moment it opened. "I swear I smell cigarettes and alcohol on him when he comes home at night, but if I dare even suggest he might be drinking, he blows up at me, shouting at me for accusing him of drinking when I know he has Hep C."

Carol's cup slips from her fingers. She grabs for it, splashing tea as she catches it. Her eyes are wide as her expression flattens.

Oh my God, Monica. He is drinking," she blurts out, sounding both pained and astonished.

"What?" I ask. "Who?"

"Steve," Carol says, putting her cup down. There's disbelief and frustration in her dark eyes as she reaches out to lay her hand on mine. "Remember when Weldon and Steve played that golf tournament last spring? Well, Steve bought a beer off the drink cart."

I snatch my hand off the table, clutching it close to my chest as I stare at Carol. I can't process what she's said. Steve bought a beer? Carol's still speaking.

"Of course, Weldon gave him hell for drinking," she says, once more cupping her hands around her tea. "Do you know what Steve did? He flat out told Weldon to mind his own business." There's outrage in her voice.

I can no more fathom the idea of Steve drinking than I can imagine Weldon tolerating being told to butt out by Steve. Weldon doesn't take shit from anyone.

"Well, when Weldon told me I immediately called Steve and chewed him out royally. Before I hung up I told him I was going to call you. He begged me not to. He promised he would tell you himself."

Carol drags in a breath, then her shoulders sag and outrage drains from her. That leaves nothing in her expression but pain. "I'm so sorry, Monica. I believed him. I mean, he called me the very next day and told me how you two had talked. He sounded so contrite, like you'd really given him what for. He told me he was done drinking forever. I am so sorry. I should have called you anyway."

I can see it in her face. She can't believe Steve's lied to her. He's lied to me, too.

If he's lied about that, what else has he lied about?

I stand up. Lunch is over. "I have to go, Carol," I say, then turn and walk away without another word.

I call Steve from my mobile phone as I walk out of the

restaurant. "Get your fucking ass home now," I shout into the phone as he answers.

He's at work. Not long ago he moved Emerald Coast Financial out of our home and into an efficiency office—a single room office that uses a shared secretary—near that damned restaurant. We arrive home at almost the same time and collide in the upstairs kitchen.

"How long have you been fucking drinking," I demand at the top of my lungs.

Steve's eyes narrow. "Oh, who have you been talking to? Carol?" His tone is snide.

His unexpected reaction punctures my anger. Steve always explodes when he's confronted. Off balance, all I can do is reply, "Yes, Carol. Tell me," I command. "How long have you been drinking?"

He makes an impatient noise and looks up at the ceiling as if he's counting. His behavior is so out of character that I shift back from him. Who is this stranger?

"Oh, for about a year now," he tells me as if it's no big deal.

All of a sudden I know what it's like to parent a resentful teen. My kid just happens to be able to write big checks and has Hepatitis C.

Steve stands with his hand on his hip, lounging casually against the kitchen counter as if he hasn't a care in the world. I stare at him, my life folding in on me, collapsing like a house of cards, dropping spade by spade until there's nothing left of my whole world. I clutch my chest. My heart hurts so much I wonder if I'm having a heart attack. I take deep breaths until the pain begins to ebb.

"Are you telling me you drank through all your Interferon treatment?"

"Yeah. So?"

His smart-alecky tone drives me over the edge. I'm beyond speaking or even thinking. Wheeling, I kick the nearest cabinet with all my might. The wooden door bounces against the frame. It feels so good I do it again and again until my foot begins to hurt.

Panting in rage and exertion, I whirl on him. "Seven hundred and fifty fucking dollars a month. You might as well have flushed that money down the toilet. I can't believe you let me continue to give you useless injections when you knew how upset I was about having needles in our house!"

I'll never forget how lost I felt staring at the box of syringes with their fine needles when we brought them home with the Interferon. I never thought I'd have needles and syringes in this house, my Clean house.

"I can't believe I had to hear from a friend that you're drinking," I continue.

No, what I can't believe is that he's deceived me and destroyed our future because he wanted a drink.

Unconsidered words come pouring out of me. "All those walks, all those grilled chicken dinners and watching the calories! What the fuck is wrong with you?" I shout. "Why am I fighting harder for your life than you are?"

He shrugs, still nonchalant. "Monica, don't you get it? It doesn't matter what I do. I'm going to die. I told you. If I'm going to die, I'm going to do whatever the fuck I want to until it happens."

My anger dies, sizzling into fear as I understand why he's not exploding at me. Before, back when we were using, Steve always followed his drinks with drugs because he didn't like the way alcohol made him feel.

Fuck me. If he's drinking, he must be drugging. The nightmare is back.

I stare up at him. "I have to know. What drugs are you doing?"

He looks at me as if I'm the crazy one. "I'm not doing any drugs. I'm just drinking," he retorts. He almost seems insulted by my question.

My stomach clenches. He's lied about everything else, why not about this? "I just need to ask you one more thing.

Do you think you're an alcoholic?"

Steve frowns a little and tilts his head to one side as if seriously contemplating my question. "No, I really don't think I am. It's drugs I have the problem with, not alcohol."

I can hardly believe he says this with a straight face after everything we've been through. This is Steve, the man who's been thrown out of bars and destroyed hotel rooms while drunk, not to mention he's had at least five DUIs. He wrecked a whole line of parked cars with the last one. Just like me, Steve comes from a long line of alcoholics. And Steve doesn't have a problem with alcohol?

"And you really believe this?" I demand, foolishly hoping for a different answer this time.

"Yes, I do," he replies.

This is the first time that I've actually witnessed the full power of denial. That's because for the first time I'm looking back at it from a place of sobriety. Just now, the enormity of Steve's denial is beyond my comprehension.

There's only one thing left to do. "You need to go back into treatment. You need to go back to Amity," I tell him.

That knocks the nonchalance right out of him. Bright color flares on his cheeks. He straightens and his fists close. "No fucking way. I'm not going through that shit again."

I'm not backing down. I can't. This is not just the rest of Steve's life, it's the rest of mine.

"Then you'll have to do an outpatient program, see Dr. Al. Attend A.A." It's not a suggestion, it's a command.

I don't expect him to agree with me. I expect him to rage and resist. I expect to fight about this for hours. I also expect to win, and I think Steve also knows I will. I think deep down he realizes how committed I am to maintaining our sobriety. No, not ours, not anymore. Just mine.

Much to my surprise, Steve relaxes, again slouching against the counter. "Okay. I'll do that."

"Are you serious?"

He shrugs. "Yeah, sure."

His unexpected agreement pulls the emotional rug out from under my feet, leaving me feeling lost and alone and completely off balance. I reach out, putting my arms around the man I love and almost fall against his chest. Tears well.

"I don't want you to die, Steve," I cry. "I'm sorry I'm being so hard on you, but I love you. I'm fighting for your life and our future."

I feel him relax against me. His arms come around me as he pulls me closer. "Oh, babe. I'm sorry."

I look up. His expression is soft. The stranger is gone. Here he is, my sweet Steve again.

He smiles at me. "Okay, I'll stop drinking. Just help me find the programs you want me to attend."

So I do. Steve starts attending an outpatient clinic in Scottsdale. His A.A. meetings are every Tuesday night.

I want to trust him. I really do, but I can't.

On the night of his third A.A. meeting, I drive by the location. His car isn't in the parking lot.


*October, 1993*
*Paradise Valley, Arizona*

"Dinner's ready," I call to Steve.

"Coming," he calls back from downstairs in the Media room where he's been watching TV.

I hear him tromp up the stairs. He joins me at the kitchen table. As we pick up our knives and forks, he asks, "How was your day?" His tone is flat, uninterested even.

"Fine," I reply, not looking up as I cut myself a bite of tonight's dinner, another meal of healthy grilled chicken. "We got a major donation for the Cancer Society Gala today. It's shaping up to be one of the best ever. How was your day?" I counter, because the conversation ball is now in my court.

"Fine," he replies.

This is how it's been ever since I learned he wasn't attending AA. I don't confront him about lying to me so he can't lie to me anymore. All I've accomplished is to make myself utterly sick and tired of everything always being fucking fine.

"Have you thought any more about taking over the checkbook?" Steve asks.

I shake my head. "You know honey, I've thought about it, but I've got so much going on right now. Now, tell me again. Why is it you want me to start doing this? I thought you liked taking care of our finances."

That's me, once again refusing to take on Steve's job in our marriage. It's his only job in our relationship and it makes me suspicious that he's even asking me about it.

"I like it fine, I just think taking care of the checkbook is something you should learn to do," he says.

That seems to exhaust all the avenues of our conversation and we fall silent. Steve's knife rasps against his plate as he cuts his chicken. I push my salad around my plate, no longer hungry.

"Monica, I've been thinking."

I look up. Steve puts a piece of chicken in his mouth and chews. I wait, brows raised. He glances at me, swallows then turns his attention back to his chicken to cut another bite.

"I think I don't want to be married anymore," he says to his plate.

I stare at the only man I've been with, the only man I've wanted to be with, for twenty-one years. I am completely unable to hear what he just said. I mean, I heard what he said. It's just that I can't believe he said it. Suddenly, I'm all for everything going back to being fucking fine.

"You what?" I ask, because it's possible he really didn't say what I just heard. I mean, it is possible I misheard him.

Not fucking probable, but possible.

He raises his gaze to meet mine. "I think I don't want to be married anymore," he repeats.

He could have been asking me to pass him the salt. There's no emotion to see in his eyes, not love, not pain, not even the anticipation of any pleasure at how his words might hurt me. He's just dead blank.

There's that dead word again.

All of a sudden I can feel my life unraveling around me. "What? You don't love me anymore? What did I do? Is the chicken not done to your liking?" This is defensive humor born of panic and it's not funny.

Steve only shakes his head. "It's not like that. I still love you. I'm just not in love with you anymore. We've been together a lot of years, you know."

He's so assured and confident. This isn't my Steve. He doesn't think like this. I'm sure someone else had to have put this idea into his head. But what if this is Steve's own thought?

My need to hold onto him is so huge that I can't face it, and the only way I know how to avoid what I don't want to see is to take charge.

"Okay, I hear you. You still love me, you're just not in love with me," I say, sounding every inch the therapist.

Years and years of participating in every sort of therapy have taught me well. "So, what's going on with you? Why aren't you in love with me anymore? You can tell me everything. I offer you complete amnesty."

I'm using a term we learned at Amity. Offering Steve amnesty is offering him freedom from consequences no matter what he's about to tell me. I'm promising I won't take his shoes or shave his fucking head.

I put my hand out to Steve. "I just need to know what's going on. Come on, let's just be honest." I pause, screwing up the courage to spit out the question that must be asked. "Are you having an affair?"

"No, of course not," he replies, still as cool as ice. His assurance falls flat. That's exactly what he told me every time I asked if he was drinking.

Steve reaches across the table and takes my hand, reeling me back into his life now that he's destroyed me. "I'm just thinking about things. Look, let's not worry about this now. Let's have our trip to Switzerland."

We're leaving on another vacation in a few days. This time Steve's attending a banking conference in Lugano, Switzerland, with Mike DeCampo, a money manager with Credite Suisse. I'm thrilled, because I don't trust Steve's present financial guy. With any luck, by the end of this conference Steve will see the light and hire Mike.

As far as Steve's concerned, we've closed the subject. And what am I supposed to do? Pretend that what just happened didn't?

Fuck, yes.

And I do. I am, after all, my parents' child. What I'm just not coming to grips with is how completely Steve is my dad and I have become my mom. I never realized how talented an actress my mother was until I started playing her role. Now, it's me pretending that real life isn't real, and me promising myself that tomorrow will be a better day.

So off Steve and I go to Lugano. After his little talk with me, I expect him to be tense or distant. He's anything but. We cuddle every morning. After Steve's daily seminars end, we walk the city streets, window-shopping and looking for just the right restaurant. We linger over our dinner until the wee hours. Steve doesn't drink, not even a drop.

It's like a second honeymoon.

No, it's like a first honeymoon. We shared our original honeymoon with another couple, one of Steve's scumbag friends and his wife who just happened to show up at the same hotel in Acapulco we were at. I wasn't thrilled, but Steve saw this supposed coincidence as an opportunity for a party. Of course, I was instantly elected hostess, which meant finding a dealer in a strange city.

Switzerland is nothing like Acapulco. By the time the conference wraps up I'm so happy I swear I glow. I can't imagine Steve ever again saying that he's not in love with me, not after the way he's acted on this trip.

And me? I'm happy to leave the past in the past. I'm positive, truly convinced, that Steve's declaration was just one of his wayward thoughts. It came and it went, and things are much better now.

The glow lingers after we get home. Steve doesn't say word one about ending our marriage. After a few weeks I stop worrying. It's so easy not to think and just keep doing what I've always done.

# CHAPTER FIFTEEN
## MR. SARLI'S SECRETARY

*November 21, 1993*
*Paradise Valley, Arizona*

The Phoenix Symphony Ball came and went. I wore St. Johns, a white satin blouse, full length black skirt and one of those great sequined belts St. Johns makes. They're stupid expensive but beautiful.

So is my new twenty thousand dollar diamond tennis bracelet Steve bought for me after we returned from Switzerland. I suspect the bracelet is a guilt gift, Steve's way of saying he's sorry for all the hurt he's caused me and our relationship. That doesn't keep me from loving it. I'm actually looking forward to wearing it home in a few days on our annual trip back to Kansas City for Thanksgiving even though Ralph and Mary Helen are sure to comment and not positively.

As I'm doing laundry, organizing our clothes so we can pack for the trip, the phone rings.

"Hello?" I say, holding the receiver against my shoulder as I fold linens.

"Is Mr. Sarli available, please?" asks the woman on the other end. When I ask who she is, she tells me she's a travel agent and names her agency. I recognize the name, because it's the one Steve uses when he books our travel. He likes them because they have online booking, something still fairly unusual.

"He's not in right now," I reply. Steve's out playing golf with Mark White today. That surprised me. Steve barely knows Mark. I guess no one else was available for a round. "Can I take a message?"

"Yes. Could you please have him call me at this number?" She gives me an 800 number. I scramble to grab a pen and my notepad to take it down.

Once I have it, I ask, "May I tell him what this is regarding?"

"Of course. Let him know we can't process the payment he made for his upcoming trip to New York on December Fifth. He's given us an incorrect credit card number."

I make a face. As much as Steve liked Mike DeCampo, he didn't move all his assets into Mike's hands. He's still got funds with that money guy in the Big Apple. That's who he's going to visit on his trip.

"I'm sorry? What's wrong with his credit card?" I ask.

"Nothing's wrong with the card. We just can't use it. His trip is booked on America West Airlines and he gave us his American Airlines credit card number to use to charge it. All we need is another card number, a Visa, MasterCard, Diner's Club or American Express."

Steve's Dyslexia strikes again. If he'd been flying United this wouldn't have happened.

I would offer the woman a credit card number now if I had one, but I don't. Steve keeps all major credit cards in his wallet; one card for each account. I have my own set of cards: Neiman's, Saks, Macy's, Dillards. If I don't have a card for the store I'm in, I write a check.

That leaves me nothing to tell the agent, except, "I'll have him call you back as soon as he gets in." She thanks me and we hang up.

That afternoon Steve gets back from golfing looking a

little tanned from being out in the sun all day. It's warm for November, with temperatures up in the mid-eighties. He looks relaxed and happy, like he's had a great time. Who knew he liked Mark White so much?

I greet him with a kiss then give him the note about his flight. He thanks me and calls the agency as I fix dinner. We have a really pleasant evening and retire for the night.

Or rather Steve retires.

I keep vampire hours. I usually don't fall asleep before two A.M. and I've been known to sleep in until noon. I channel surf until I come across a movie about a forty-year-old man in midlife crisis having an affair with a younger woman. It catches my interest, but the longer I watch the more uncomfortable I feel.

The lightning bolt hits me at the end of the picture. In that instant my denial shatters and I get a good look at what I've been refusing to see for so long.

The man in the movie is Steve. Steve's having an affair. It wasn't Mark White Steve was with today. He was with some bimbo.

The next morning after Steve leaves for the day, I go into our home office, looking for my note with the travel agency's phone number on it. I have no trouble finding it on Steve's desk.

Neatness is Steve's mechanism for dealing with his Dyslexia. The slightest bit of mess throws him, so in his office he's created a place for everything and keeps everything in its place. His file folders even have color-coded labels on them. Within moments I have my note in my hand.

Finding the courage to make the call takes me a couple of hours. When I reach the reservation agent who called yesterday, I say in my best secretarial voice, "Hi, this is Mr. Steve Sarli's secretary. You called yesterday about his flight to New York next week. I just wanted to confirm that you received the information you needed from him."

"Yes," the woman on the other end says, "we have. His

reservation is confirmed."

My heart is pounding like a sledgehammer. "Confirmed for both parties?" I ask, feeling like I'm standing outside my own body.

"Yes, for both parties," she replies.

I bite my lip to keep myself from moaning out loud. I don't know how I manage to do this, but I coolly ask, "I'd like to confirm the spelling of the second party's name."

(This isn't something I could do today, but back in pre-9/11 days flight lists weren't classified information.)

"Of course," the agent replies. "S-t-a-c-y-c-o-n-n-o-r."

Stacy Connor. There it is: her name and proof that he's having an affair.

That knife in my chest drops to my gut, slicing me in two as it goes.

"Thank you," I manage and hang up, then explode out of Steve's office chair. I pace the room, shrieking and crying.

I can only maintain that level of pain for about twenty minutes before I'm spent. As I begin to calm down, something nudges in my memory. Stacy Connor. I know that name.

Neurons fire. A moment later I wipe my face, sit back down in the chair and call the store where Steve buys his clothing.

"This is Stacy. How can I help you?"

I can't believe she answers the phone. "Hi Stacy, this is Monica Sarli."

"Oh hi Monica. How are you?"

I don't bother to respond to her query. "What's your last name?"

"My last name?" Stacy replies, sounding a little confused. "Connor. Why?"

I'm on my feet again, on fire with righteous outrage and just plain rage. "Stay the fuck away from my husband!" I scream into the phone and slam down the receiver only to snatch it back up to dial Steve.

"Get your ass home now!" I shout at him when he answers.

He's in the door a few minutes later, his mobile phone still pressed to his ear.

I'm a dragon. I fucking breathe fire.

No, I'm much farther gone than that. I'm fucking Naya on a rampage. I'm putting Steve's ass on the bus and then I'm shaving his head.

"Tell your girlfriend to hang up. You need to talk to your wife now." The beams in the roof shudder at the force of my command.

Oh yeah, I'm definitely Naya.

His phone snaps shut. He looks like a little boy caught with his hand in the cookie jar.

"Who are you taking to New York on December fifth?" I demand, my voice cool and flat.

"No one," he squeaks.

I cannot believe this. He's still trying to lie even though he knows I've called his bimbo. "Try again. Who are you taking to New York with you?"

"I'm going alone," he stutters out.

"No!" I shout. "Tell me the truth. Who are you taking with you?"

"No one," he says one more time.

"You are not going alone!" I scream. "I called the travel agency. I know you're not traveling alone."

His expression flattens in shock, then his eyes widen in panic. "They're lying!" he tries to shout back, but his voice breaks as he speaks.

Does he really think I'm that stupid or is he just that desperate to escape the truth?

"You are going to New York with Stacy Connor!" I scream. It's not possible to lower my voice.

As Steve hears me say her name he turns white as a sheet. He's trapped and he knows it. There's no lie left that can save him.

"I'm not dealing with this shit," he cries, sounding for all the world like a scared child. He pivots and bolts out the door.

Yep. My life is unraveling like a badly knitted sweater and there's nothing I can do to stop it.

Steve returns home a few hours later. He's so upset he's shaking. He looks like shit.

I can't look much better, although I doubt Steve can see me. I'm sitting in the dark at the kitchen table, pretty much convinced I'm in shock. Either that or I've turned into a statue, because I can't feel a thing.

I have new empathy for Mary Helen.

Actually, it's not true that I can't feel. There are two things I'm sensing. The first is shame. I'm fucking wallowing in it. I'm terrified of what people will think of me when they find out my husband is cheating on me. I can't bear to face our families. I've spent too long practicing honesty as part of my sobriety to stay in the Sarlis' guest room over Thanksgiving and not tell them what's happening with Steve. Steve might be able to hide this disaster from them, but I can't.

I'm so screwed. And trapped, because the second thing I'm feeling is determination.

Deep within me is the certainty that I can and will save my marriage. I have to. My dad always told me I wasn't a quitter and I still believe him. Plus, even though I'm not a practicing Catholic, when I married Steve I married him for better or worse, until death do us part.

I promised and so did he.

None of that even begins to take into consideration the fact that Steve is still the love of my life, even if he's cheated on me. There's no one else I want to be with, not even now.

I look up at Steve, knowing that if I'm committed to

keeping my marriage whole, then I must remain calm at all costs. The only thing explosions, screaming and shouting will do is drive Steve into running again.

Whatever it takes, I tell myself as Steve turns on the light, I'm saving my marriage.

He sits in a chair at the opposite side of the table. I can't bear to look at him.

"Okay. This is the deal," he says to me, his voice quavering a little, "I want to stay married to you and keep our life the way it is, but I also want to keep my girlfriend and the apartment."

That gets my attention. I stare at him. Fuck me. This is outrageous. He has an apartment? There's only one response I can make.

"Okay, that's fine with me."

I mean, really. Didn't I just tell myself whatever it takes? Then, what the fuck else is there for me to say?

But I'm not a total welcome mat, so I add, "I'll give you what you want, but here's what I want. You pay for everything. That includes everything I want and whatever she costs you. I'm your wife. I'm not taking a pay cut."

I think my instant agreement surprises him, because he perks right up. "Okay, we can do that."

With that, he's all grins and chuckles. He comes to his feet, presses a kiss to my forehead, turns and practically runs from our house.

And I realize he's hurrying off to go tell her.

Forget fuck me. Fuck him!

What the fuck am I supposed to do about our trip home for Thanksgiving?

I'm feeling so small that I don't know what else to do but go to bed. A few hours later I hear the front door open. I start toward the door and meet Steve in the living room. He looks like shit, worn and beat up. Dark circles mark his eyes. His hair, worn longer these days, looks unkempt and dirty. I can tell he's been drinking.

"I'm not going to Kansas City for Thanksgiving," he says.

"Fine, then you call your parents and tell them that," I say.

Stark terror fills his face. "No," he whispers.

I shake my head. "I'm done. This is where it stops, Steve. I won't lie or cover up for you anymore. You're going to call your parents right now and you're going to tell them everything you've been doing."

Monica the Cleaner has just quit her job.

He blinks at me. The quiet stretches. "I think we need to call Bette," he says. "I'm in too deep. I can't figure this out on my own. I need help."

Well, that's something I totally agree with, but I don't believe for an instant Steve really wants to go back to Amity. I'm not that stupid. He just doesn't want to face his dad.

"You'll go back to Amity?" I ask, pushing him a little. I want him to admit out loud how big a coward he is. Bette's always called him the ball-less wonder.

"I will. I'll go this very night," Steve replies, his words falling out of his mouth so fast they almost bump into mine. "I'll go right now."

I pick up the phone and call Bette. I've pretty much got her on speed dial these days. We've been talking more frequently ever since Carol exposed Steve's drinking.

When Bette gets on the phone I tell her that Steve's in bad shape and he wants to come down to Amity. "Put him on the phone," she commands me.

I listen to Steve's side of the conversation. "Yeah, I'm fucked up. Drinking again. Okay, I'll come down there."

My spider sense buzzes. This is all too easy.

Steve hands me the phone. "Bette wants to talk to you."

As I take the phone from him, Steve slumps back. His head hangs. He looks like he doesn't have an ounce of energy left in him.

"Well Monica, he's still lying, isn't he?" Bette says with no lack of cynicism in her voice. I don't say anything, because admitting Steve's been lying is also admitting that I've been willing to live in denial so I don't have to confront his lying.

Bette continues. "So, he wants to come down here again. Interesting. Go ahead and bring him. I'll see if I can get him to talk. How about you? Are you okay? Are you staying clean?"

"Yes!" I fill the word with all the power of my continuing sobriety.

God, it's good to hear me confirm that I'm keeping the promise I made to myself. I feel its truth fill me. Drinking and drugging are no longer an option for me, no matter what happens to me. Clean and sober just happens to be the way I'll live out the rest of my life, no matter the pain.

The sense of accomplishment and elation lasts a nano-second, and then collapses beneath my shame. It takes all my courage to add, "He's having an affair." My voice shakes with embarrassment.

There's silence on the line for a minute. "Remember in 1984 at your interview?" Bette asks me, her voice suddenly soft.

I shift the phone against my ear. "I remember."

How could I ever forget? Bette and Naya had interviewed Steve first then called me in. I sat in a straight-backed chair in their office while the two of them rocked in their rockers as we discussed why I wanted to be at Amity. The answer was simple: I didn't have anywhere else to go.

As the interview wrapped up, Bette leaned forward in her rocker. "I think you should know Steve's told us the only reason he's coming to Amity is to support you in cleaning up. Steve says you have a drug problem, he doesn't."

"He uses as much as I do," I protested.

They both laughed. "You think we don't know that? You think we can't see his arms? That man's got tracks from his fingers to his elbows," Naya said. Naya is a beautiful woman, with deep brown hair, even features and piercing ice-blue eyes. Her thick silver cuff bracelet almost hides the tattoo of entwined snakes on the inside of her wrist.

Then Bette added, "Monica, Steve's a liar. He lies about everything and that will never change. Hear me now; his lying will be his downfall."

Now, as I listen on the phone, Bette says, "Do you also remember Naya and me telling you then that we thought you'd make it and he wouldn't?"

I haven't been able to forget that even though I've tried. I hated hearing it back then as much as I hate hearing it now. Fuck me, I was so certain I was strong enough to clean up for both of us.

"Yes," I manage reluctantly.

"Yeah, well it's good you still remember that. Now you listen to me. Nothing has changed. Steve is still a liar. He's always been a liar and he will always be a liar. Hold onto that and bring him down tomorrow," she continues. "Once he's here, we'll see what happens."

"Okay," I reply, not quite listening and not in the least comforted.

Once the line is clear, I again hand the phone to Steve. "If you're going to Amity tomorrow we really have to call your parents. They need to know you're not coming for Thanksgiving. I can't just show up without you."

Steve again turns white. He pushes the phone back toward me, the gesture almost pleading. "Why should I be the one to call them?"

I see it in his eyes. He can't believe I'm deserting him and the job I do in our relationship.

I stand my ground. Not even to save my marriage can I do this for him. Besides didn't he desert me first? Steve's betrayal is too huge and hurts too much.

"No, it ends here. You're the one who isn't going to be there for Thanksgiving. You're the one who has to tell them."

Steve hesitates. In his eyes I watch his disbelief give way to a flicker of resentment.

What? Did he think I liked groveling in front of Ralph for him? I don't bother saying anything. Instead, I tell myself I'm a boulder, immovable and massive. Steve will give in before I do.

And he does. His shoulders sag. He takes the phone and dials his parents' number. Our house is so quiet I can hear the faint sound of their phone ringing when it echoes out of the receiver.

"Hi Mom," Steve says a moment later, sounding miserable. He listens for a minute. "Mom, I'm not coming home for Thanksgiving."

Another pause. "Ah, um, I'm in trouble again. I need some help. I decided to go back into treatment. That's why I'm not coming."

Still another pause. He wordlessly hands the phone to me. Old habits die hard. It's all fine for me to tell Steve to speak for himself, but that only works if his parents are willing to listen to him and they don't even know they're supposed to. They're too accustomed to me doing the talking.

I take the phone. "Hello?"

"Monica, what the hell is going on there?" Mary Helen demands.

"Well," I say, and all of the sudden the ground is again firm beneath my feet. Maybe I'm trying to change too fast on a day when I've already experienced too many new and painful things. "Steve's been having an affair with a sales girl. And, he's been drinking again. I just found out about it."

"But is he using drugs?" Mary Helen's voice is clipped and sharp.

I'm taken aback for a second until I remember. Steve's drinking doesn't mean anything to her or Ralph. It never has, no matter how much they paid to clean up his messes.

For them, consuming alcohol is part of what everyone does, a real family tradition. It's another reminder that I'm the one who's changed, the one now accustomed to living without an addiction.

That is, unless I consider Steve might be my biggest addiction.

All of a sudden, Ralph's on the extension. "What's happening? Steve is using drugs again?"

"I don't know," I reply with a sigh. "He's just so messed up right now. I'm going to take him down to Amity tomorrow. I'm not staying with him. I'll be in Kansas City on Wednesday as we planned. We'll talk then."

There's no space for small talk after that. Mary Helen sort of grunts her agreement. "See you on Wednesday, then," Ralph says and they hang up.

Steve and I go to bed. Together. In the same bed.

Nothing has changed. Nothing has changed. Nothing has changed.

It's my new mantra. I think I'm still chanting it come dawn. I'm surely chanting it as he packs his bag and we set off for Tucson.

If you've never done it, the drive from Phoenix to Tucson on I-10 has to be one of the most boring in the country. There's nothing between Arizona's two major cities except scrubby Mesquite trees, the occasional pecan orchard, a few saguaro cactuses and flat, dusty land. Not sand, our deserts don't have any sand, just gravelly dirt.

We listen to a Sting tape for most of the trip and take turns crying. While I'm sobbing Steve does his best to reassure me that everything will be all right. He's lying again. We both know nothing will ever be the same.

Amity's gatekeeper meets us just as I expect, and finds Steve's name on his clipboard. We pass through the gate to the facility's inner sanctum. It's all just the way it was when we were here the first time. Outside of Bette's office, Steve takes his place on The Pew, which is just what its name suggests: a wooden bench seat from some old church; Bette and Naya have dark and twisted senses of humor. As he removes his shoes as instructed, Bette comes out of her office. She looks the same as she did almost ten years ago, like an up-scale suburban housewife not like the bad-ass dragon bitch she is. Relief flows through me. Steve is safe here. I'm certain Bette will find a way to fix this.

She better, because I sure the fuck can't figure out what to do.

She hands Steve a pen and notebook. "Okay, asshole," she barks, "start writing down your dirt, all the stuff you've done that you know isn't right. When you're finished we'll see what we can do with you."

Bette walks me back out to the parking lot. "Why do you think he agreed to come back here? He didn't put up any fight. You both hated it here," she says to me when we're standing beside my car.

I want so badly to say it's because Steve wants to get well. I don't bother. I might be living in denial and lying to myself, but I know better than to lie to Bette.

"Because he'd rather be here at Amity than face his family?" I offer tentatively.

Bette smiles in approval. "You win the gold star."

The next day I'm in Kansas City. It isn't easy to sit in my in-laws living room and tell them about Steve's affair and his drinking. It's so hard to confront the rottenness I've suddenly realized is eating at the foundation of my happily ever after, the life that I wanted them to be so proud of.

Mary Helen looks as beautiful as ever, dressed in full armor, perfectly made up and not a hair out of place. There's a half empty tumbler in her hand. I don't see any sign of it in her expression, but I know she must be as devastated by Steve's fall from functioning as Ralph is. Or me.

"You know, Monica, all men go through this phase, es-pecially at Steve's age," she tells me, not unkindly. "They stray a little, have a little fun, but they come back. You just need to let this thing with the shop girl run its course. He'll get tired of her and come back. He loves you."

It's in her voice. She absolutely believes Steve loves me and for that I'm immensely grateful. In the next second I absorb what she's just said and her meaning startles me.

I glance from her to Ralph, wondering if Mary Helen is speaking from experience.

Ralph tears up the way he always does when thinking about his screwup son. "What's wrong with him, Monica," he pleads with me.

Oh, let me name the things wrong with Steve. For starters there's the brain damage done by the shock therapy he had at fifteen for depression after he lost his first girlfriend. How about he's fucking disabled with Dyslexia and has a fifth grade reading level? What about his years of drinking, Heroin abuse, not to mention Crack Cocaine? And let's not forget that he's dying of Hepatitis C. There's almost nothing right with Steve.

"I think it's the Hep C," I reply, glancing between them, choosing the one thing wrong with Steve that doesn't in any way reflect back on them. All I've ever wanted to do since cleaning up is make these two people proud. It kills me that I have to hurt them this way. I love Steve's parents. I think I'm closer to them than I am my own parents.

"I'm doing everything I can to keep him healthy," I continue, "but he fights me every step of the way. I keep telling him this illness doesn't have to be a death sentence, but he's got it in his head he's done for."

All of a sudden I remember an afternoon a few weeks back. Steve hadn't been to the gym, so I started in on him, insisting that he walk with me. The more he resisted, the louder I got until I was almost shouting at him before he finally got his shoes on and went with me. In that instant I picture myself the way Steve must, as the Nazi health spa bitch, standing over him with a whip, forcing him to do what I believe is good for him when he doesn't think anything he does will make a difference.

Why wouldn't he go looking for some other woman, someone who'll let him do what he wants?

My eyes close as I start to sink into despair. What happened to us? Where's that perfect life we were supposed to be living, the one I was building for both of us?

"What can we do?" Ralph wants to know.

"I don't know," I say and that's the whole truth. I really don't know what to do nor do I have any of my usual half-baked plans of how to save Steve this time.

The next day we're halfway through our turkey dinner when Bette calls. "The asshole's run off," she tells me. "I put him in group after he wrote me a few pages of bullshit. I told him it was time to finally come clean. He won't do it, Monica. I'm sorry. Call me when you hear from him."

I hang up. All hope, and there were still grains of it hiding deep within me, is gone. I tell my in-laws.

"What do you mean he's gone? Where would he go?" Ralph wants to know.

The only place I can imagine he would go is to HER, but I don't know where SHE is. Instead, I start calling, his friends, his restaurant, our neighbors, Dick and Lilli. I'm almost out of numbers when something jingles in my memory. A hairdresser at my hair salon had seen Steve at a party the previous summer. I'd been in Europe with a friend at the time. I call the guy who hosted it and strike gold. He tells me that he picked Steve up from the Phoenix bus station and took him home.

To our house.

What an idiot I am. Of course Steve is still running to me. I'm the one who always fixes things for him. He still needs me.

And that makes me angry. I forget that I'm committed to saving our marriage no matter what. I won't clean up for Steve this time. This time, he has to clean up for himself.

I call the house. When Steve answers, I shout, "Why

the fuck did you run away? They were going to help you."

"There's nothing wrong with me. I don't have a prob-lem," he retorts indignantly.

My breath catches as I realize I'm just playing the Nazi bitch again. What good is shouting when he's not listening? So, I stop. Completely. Silence echoes over the phone line as the seconds tick by.

Once again, Steve gives way first. "Monica, I can't do it. I don't want to live with criminals again. I don't want to go back to digging ditches."

Neither do I. That's why I stay clean. It's why I never lie about my past, and always tell people where I've been and what I've done. It's why I work so hard at my charities.

That's when it hits me. Steve hasn't done any of these things. I'm the only one not lying about our past. Oh, Steve will smile and nod when I tell our story, but I can't remember once when he actually spoke the words *I am a recovering addict* out loud.

This realization is so stunning that I tell Steve I won't cut short my visit to Kansas City. I'm staying until Sunday as originally planned. I need every minute of that time to absorb how completely delusional I've been.

When I arrive home on Sunday Steve's not there. He shows up a few hours later looking fucked up and dirty, like he hasn't showered or shaved since he ran from Amity.

No, he looks like a homeless man, a dying homeless man.

My heart aches.

"What's going on, Steve?" I beg him.

All he says before he goes to bed is, "Call Bette. I want to go back to Amity."

So I do. Bette says, "Bring him back."

We make the trip the next day, on the thirtieth of No-vember. On the first of December, he calls me from a motel in Tucson.

"Please Monica, I want to come home now. I'm taking

the bus. Pick me up at the station. Please," he pleads with me.

Fuck. I can't do this anymore. As much as I love Steve, this has to end and I'm the only one who can do it.

"I'll pick you up, but you can't stay here. Steve, I'm clean and I want to stay that way. As long as you're using drugs and alcohol you're a threat to my sobriety and it's not an option for you to come back and live in this house."

Tears fill my eyes as I speak these words. With all our fights, drugging, screaming, dramas and the rest, this is the hardest thing I've ever done. I love Steve but I'm sick with grief over what he's become. I'm even more terrified that he'll once again tell me our marriage is over and I'll lose him.

That's when it hits me. I've already lost Steve. I haven't lost him to HER as much as I've lost him to his addictions.

I hear Steve sniffle. "Then what am I supposed to do?" he asks.

"You have to find another treatment center." There's no sign of pain in my voice. I'm back on firm ground again, at least for the moment. I know exactly what I need to do—have to do—to give Steve the chance to step into our future with me.

"Let me come home. Help me find me somewhere to go." He sounds like a child, a little lost boy.

I sigh. We've been together for decades. This is the man I gave my virginity to. There's nothing else for me to say, except, "Come home, then. But you will be living some-where else within two days."

What I find for him is The Meadows, an internationally renowned addiction treatment center. It's located in Wicken-burg, Arizona, a small town sixty miles northwest of Phoenix. And two days later I drive him to the center. He commits himself for the full month of December.

The coward still doesn't have the balls to face his fam-ily.

# CHAPTER SIXTEEN
## MINDING MY
## P'S AND Q'S

*December, 1993*
*Paradise Valley, Arizona*

My phone rings. I stir uneasily in bed, and then glance at the clock and groan. It's eleven in the morning; I only fell asleep at seven. I haven't been able to sleep much since Steve's commitment to The Meadows. All I can think about is how he's ruined our happily ever after.

The phone continues to ring. Whoever's on the other end isn't giving up.

I sit up and squint. I don't much care for draperies or window coverings. Instead, I have shutters. The wide slats are partially open.

Sunbeams find golden tones in my off white carpeting. Standing directly across from me is my armoire. Built to my design, well mine and Carol's, it's distressed oak, but doesn't look it. Instead it wears a coat of golden toned crackle finish that lends it spectacular depth and texture. My taupe linen and silk spread lies in heavy folds across my feet, the threads glistening in the light.

I've tossed the decorative pillows on the floor at my bedside. There's no reason not to; Mario died last year.

I feel so empty. My dog's dead and my husband's run

away. How much worse can it get?

The phone is still ringing. I finally give in and pick it up. "Hello?" My voice sounds like I feel, flat and hopeless.

"It's Sue," my friend Sue Cummings says. "I thought I'd come by and take you to lunch before our meeting this afternoon."

I groan. Even the concept of perking up enough to do lunch is beyond me at the moment. Each day since I sent Steve away has been a battle between shame and my commitments. As little as I want to face the people in my life right now, I'm still co-chair of that Cancer Gala, and the event's now only two months away. I have work to do.

"Not today, Sue. I'll see you at the meeting. I'm not up for lunch."

It's a lie, but saying that is better than telling her the truth, which is: I thought I'd stay in this afternoon and contemplate slitting my wrists.

"I'm coming over right now. Call the guard and tell him to let me in," Sue says in a voice that brooks no resistance.

Most of the time these days I feel like I'm sleepwalking and this is no different. I agree. After she hangs up, I notify the Clearwater Hills guard station she's on her way then prepare for her arrival. She lives less than a mile from me, but by the time she arrives I've showered and brushed my teeth. I meet her at my door wearing my robe.

Sue steps in, as tall, blonde and beautiful as always. Like me, Sue loves St. Johns and today she looks fabulous in a red knit suit.

She stares at me for a moment then gives an impatient huff. "You look like death warmed over. Come on."

She grabs me by the arm and leads me back through my bedroom to my bathroom. The floor in here is tumbled Limestone that gleams pale gray beneath the deep red and blue oriental carpet runner. A mirrored display case built into the wall next to my roomy snail shower contains my collection of jewel toned glass perfume bottles.

Her hands now on my shoulders, Sue turns me toward the vanity. It's topped with Travertine. The muted gold color of the walls brings out the same tones from the countertop. Just beyond the sinks is the area set aside as my dressing table.

That's where Sue takes me, pushing me down onto my antique vanity stool covered in red, gold and taupe Fortuny fabric. I'm facing the mirror. Sue stands behind me, her hands on her hips and her jaw as square as any drill sergeant's.

"Hair," she barks as she stares at me in the mirror.

I dutifully pull out my blow dryer and style my hair. Once I finish, I put away the dryer and start to rise.

"Oh no you don't," Sue says, pressing me back down onto the stool. "Now it's time for makeup."

"I don't feel like putting on makeup," I whine, finally feeling alive enough to stand up for myself.

"Monica, you're not getting this," Sue replies sternly, crossing her arms in front of her. "In our world it's all about looking good. That means you never, ever walk out your front door looking anything less than your best, no matter how bad you feel."

"But I can't face everyone," I admit, my voice barely louder than a whisper.

Tears fill my eyes and start running down my cheeks. I wipe at them in surprise. Until now I've been too overwhelmed and depressed to actually cry about what's happening to me.

"Yes you can, and you will," she retorts, but she now sounds less like a drill sergeant and more like my friend Sue.

"You have to face them," she continues more gently, "and you have to do it with a smile on your face. Every time you look sad or beaten out there," she points to the outer wall of my house, "he wins again, and you cannot let him win. Don't you get it? As long as you hide in your house, he wins.

"I wasn't going to do this yet, but maybe it will help." Sue goes into the bedroom. When she returns she has my cordless phone pressed to her ear. "Hold on a second. I have Monica right here."

When I put the phone to my ear, her husband Larry says, "Hi, Monica."

Why am I talking to Larry? I mumble something that passes for a greeting.

"I want to apologize to you." Larry sounds humble, not like his usual blustery, Ralph and Larry Kramden self. "I would never have introduced her to Steve if I'd known this would happen."

It takes me a moment to remember it was Larry who first took Steve to the big and tall store where SHE works. It's where Larry shops. Shame washes over me like a filthy wave. Larry knew what Steve was doing before I did. How could I have been so blind?

"Honestly, I didn't know Steve would do this," he adds, his voice rising a notch. "I just thought he'd loan her the money."

"What money?" I ask, and all of a sudden I can't understand why I wanted to hide. What I really need is to know everything, every fucking little detail about how Steve betrayed me, even though I know hearing it will make me sick.

"When she asked me if I knew anyone who'd loan her the money to buy a motorcycle, I just thought. . ." Larry pauses then starts again. "Well, I mean, Steve's always willing to give people. . . I'm just sorry, Monica. I had no idea this would happen."

He makes an irritable sound. "I tell you, as soon as I see Steve I'm going to let him know what an idiot he is. And you have my word that I'll tell him to come home to you. She's only using him." He sounds more like himself this time.

I tell Larry thanks, turn off the phone and set it on the

vanity top. I look in the mirror at my friend and demand, "Did you know?"

"I didn't have a clue until you told me," she assures me. "And I don't think Larry put it all together until after I told him what was happening."

She again puts her hands on her hips, holding my gaze with hers. "Now it's time to talk about divorce," she says.

"I'm not divorcing Steve," I insist, my words coming so fast they nearly bump into hers.

Sue puts a hand on my shoulder as if to reassure me. "That may be true, and for your sake I hope it is. But if it isn't, then you have to be prepared. I couldn't live with myself if something happened and he left you with nothing."

"Oh," I breathe, just now remembering that Sue's had a few husbands in her day. More to the point, she's had a few divorces, profitable divorces. Profitable for her, that is.

She's not the only woman in my acquaintance who's made a career of marrying well, trading up for older and richer each time.

There's no lack of dark amusement in the smile she offers me. "Now fix your makeup while I tell you what you need to know."

The Sue Cummings School of Divorce has just enrolled its first and most reluctant student.

"There are some rules that you must follow," she informs me. "Number one, you never leave the house looking less than your absolute best. This is critical. If you look like a mess, you'll be a mess. Rule number two, no cross words. Not ever. From this moment on, you're the sweetest person your husband has ever dealt with.

"Rule number three, always smile." She shoots me her finest smile in the mirror as if in demonstration.

"You smile no matter what anyone says, no matter how hurt you might feel about what they say. No matter what. You smile until it hurts to keep smiling."

She puts her forefingers to her cheeks and holds up

the corners of her mouth. It's more grimace than smile this time. I put away my eye liner as she lowers her hands and sends me a stern look.

"The next rule is going to be hard for you."

I start coating one eyelid with mauve shadow, still watching her in the mirror. What could be fucking harder than dealing with Steve and having to smile at everyone when I don't want to?

"Rule four," she says, "is to never, ever mention the girl-friend."

I almost choke. How can Sue know that every time I stand in my shower I imagine telling Steve—okay, maybe telling is too gentle a word—how the only thing SHE wants from him is his money?

Sue holds up a warning finger. "Never ever. Not once, Monica. You're going to do this with dignity, and screaming at him about his girlfriend isn't dignified. Besides, every time you say anything negative about her to him, you sound like a bitch and she starts to look even more attractive. So never go there."

I nod, but I'm still not ready to accept this rule. Sue's right. Number four is going to be a hard one for me. I finish with the shadow and start on mascara.

"Finally, rule number five. You need to mind your P's and Q's," Sue says.

"P's and Q's?" I frown up at her. "What does that mean?"

Her grin is wicked. "It means that if there's going to be a divorce, you're going to make sure you know absolutely every detail of Steve's finances and his business so you can soak him to the last penny. That means you have to look at everything, Monica. You need that checkbook."

Sue was shocked when I told her I had no idea how much money Steve had in his accounts. She thinks I'm fool-ish for refusing to take over the household accounting. It's not how she runs her life.

"Just remember, Monica," she tells me, sounding like Bette for an instant, "knowledge is power. Get that checkbook."

"All right," I tell her.

Much to my surprise I suddenly don't feel so defeated. I'm not sure I'm ready to face the world, but I'm certain I won't be spending any more time hiding in my bed.

Once again Sue's hands are on her hips. "No, you'll do better than that. When exactly will you know how much money is in all of Steve's account?" she demands.

"How about tonight?" I reply. She looks startled. I offer a watery smile. "Steve gave me the key to his new office. He wants me to check his phone messages and mail while he's in treatment."

God, it feels like shit to say *in treatment*. It feels worse to contemplate going through Steve's files. It feels like I'm invading his privacy. I've never once poked through his drawers or even opened his wallet without his permission. I never thought I had to. Then again, I never thought he'd hide things from me.

It's obvious Sue doesn't feel that way. She winks at me. "I hope there's a copy machine you can use. Every detail," she reminds me.

Ready to dress for lunch, I start to rise from the stool. One more time, Sue pushes me back down. "Not yet," she says. "Lipstick."

I look at her in surprise. "What about it?"

"You never leave the house without lipstick," she says. "Even if you don't have any other makeup on, you make sure you put on some goddamn lipstick. Honestly, Monica. You've got to get that in our world it's all about looking good!"

"Fuck me," I whisper to myself.

I'm sitting at Steve's desk in his little efficiency office. Up until a moment ago I was still feeling like an invader. That sense was so strong that I waited until everyone else had left this area to come here. Now, I'm fucking sorry I came.

I look down into the narrow top desk drawer as the condom packets jammed into it spill out into my lap. It's a tiny waterfall of VD prevention. My stomach heaves. I clap my hand over my mouth to keep my dinner where it belongs. Never again can I hide in denial about Steve cheating on me.

As the condoms shift the corner of a piece of paper appears. I pull it from the drawer, dislodging even more little foil squares. It's a list of phone numbers all with Nevada's area code.

Before I reconsider, I grab the phone and dial the first number. An answering machine responds.

"Hi, this is Tanya," a woman's recorded voice croons into my ear. "I'm not in right now, but leave me a message and I'll get back to you just as soon as I can."

I dial the next number. "Hi, this is Deena," another sexy sounding woman's recorded voice informs me. I don't wait to hear the rest of her message, just dial the next number.

"Hi, this is Vickie." Just the whiskey growl of this woman's voice is enough to guarantee me a good time.

Tears fill my eyes. Steve's betrayed me and betrayed me and betrayed me. My hands start to shake. The quivering moves up my arms and farther until my whole body is trembling, until I feel like I'll rattle into tiny little pieces and die if I don't stop it right now.

Once again I grab the phone and punch in a number. I'm not really conscious of who I've called until he answers.

"Jim Schlesing."

I breathe a sigh of relief. This is exactly who I need to talk to, someone completely normal, a man who totally loves and respects his wife, the sort of husband who would never cheat on the woman he loves, or if he did would make certain that no one ever found out.

"Jim, it's Monica Sarli," I say. Even my voice is quivering now. "I'm at Steve's office. I came down to check his mail for him," I start, but my voice breaks.

I gasp for air. "There are condoms everywhere," I whisper into the phone. It's how I feel, like I'm drowning in a sea of condoms.

"Oh Monica," Jim says, his voice softening in compassion. "I'm so sorry. Are you okay?"

He doesn't blame me for Steve's misbehavior. I hear it in his tone. Jim knows who I am and likes me, despite my husband.

He's given me exactly what I needed to hear. The trembling stops. I begin reassembling the bits and pieces that are me, hoping I'll someday be whole again.

"I will be," I sigh, wiping my face and sniffling a little.

Then, because I'm a glutton for punishment, I do to him what I've done to everyone since my conversation with Larry Cummings. "About Steve. Did you know what he was doing?"

The uncomfortable pause that follows my question tells me more than I want to know.

"Beth and I are so sorry this has happened to you," Jim begins. "You know, when we first met Steve we thought he was a great guy. We never expected him to go off the deep end this way. Now, I'm not telling you this next bit to hurt you, I just think you should know how bad things got. A while back I ran into Steve at Fashion Square," he says, naming Scottsdale's most upscale mall. "He was coming out of Victoria's Secret. He made a point of showing off the sexy lingerie he'd bought for his girlfriend."

"He told you he bought them for his girlfriend?" I'm shocked. This time embarrassment joins the shame that's already living inside my soul.

"He did. I was so taken aback. Why would he do something like that? I really don't know him the way I know you. I just couldn't believe how inappropriate it was. I think The Meadows is the right place for him, Monica. He's way out of control. I only hope his stay there makes a difference for him," Jim finishes kindly.

There isn't much more to say after that. Steve's been making a fool out of himself, and dragging me along with him. I wish Jim a pleasant evening and go back to searching Steve's office. What else is there for me to do?

In another drawer I find Steve's business checkbook, the kind with stubs containing information about each check. I page through those stubs, reading every one. He's written checks to casinos and companies whose names suggest they can only be escort services. I even find the eight thousand dollar check he wrote to HER for her motorcycle.

What's missing is actual business income. Emerald Coast Financial has a whole lotta money going out and nothing coming in. The only deposits are transfers from his trust.

I stare at this, understanding why Steve gave me his key. There are no checks in the mail for me to take care of for him. And it's not like Steve hasn't heard Ralph call me The Detective because I always unravel the mystery. No, when Steve gave me his key it was his way of inviting me to discover what he's really been doing because he didn't have the balls to tell me to my face.

With that in mind I have no qualms about warming up the copy machine. It takes me two nights, but when I'm done I have a copy of every tax record, every brokerage and bank statement, every check stub, every single sheet of paper in Steve's office. I stuff the copies into big manila envelopes, and then fill record boxes with the envelopes. These I take to Lilli's house to store for me.

*December 29, 1993*
*Paradise Valley, Arizona*

"Hey, babe. Would you do me a favor?" Steve asks. He's calling me from The Meadows. He's just told me he's coming home on January first. "After my group's graduation, a few of us are going to celebrate by spending New Year's

Eve together. Would you mind making us a reservation at that place we stayed at in Sedona a while back? What's it called?"

"You mean the Junipine Lodge?" I reply, speaking sweetly. Rule number two. Be the sweetest person your husband has ever dealt with.

"Yeah, that's the place!" Steve sounds totally pleased with himself.

"Sure, I'll do that," I reply. My teeth are dissolving, there's so much sugar in my voice.

The minute he hangs up I dial his counselor at The Meadows. "So, what do you know about Steve and some of your other patients planning to spend New Year's Eve together?" I ask.

"I know they're all being released, but I don't know about any plans to spend New Year's Eve together," she says to me, sounding confused.

"You're right. You don't have any fucking clue, do you?" I retort, making no attempt to soften the angry, sarcastic edge to my voice.

I hate this bitch and all the rest of the counselors up there. None of them have listened to anything I've told them about Steve. Instead, they've treated me as the enemy from the first, like the nasty Synanon bitch who's going to scare the fuck out of Steve and force the rest of their patients into a psycho-drama.

I'm sure Steve went into this treatment center telling them that I'm the one with the problem, just like he did at Amity.

"After a month of your bullshit counseling at five thousand dollars a week, Steve's still a fucking liar. Jesus, over family week he made so many promises and pretty speeches while I was there you'd have fucking thought he was running for president. Everything he said was a lie. He's still lying and you still have no fucking clue.

"What kind of Heroin addict were you anyway?" That's

what she claims, anyway. "Did you stay locked up in your house or only use in the suburbs? Didn't you lie, cheat, steal or manipulate to support your habit like the rest of us or were you some unique Dope Fiend?"

Addicts always think they're unique. We're not. I was no different from the convicts at Amity or the addicts who lived on the streets and ate out of dumpsters.

"Now Mrs. Sarli, that's your reality," the counselor says patronizingly. "You need to get some help."

She's said this to me from the first day. It makes me want to go up there, pull her out of her office and kick her fucking ass.

It's more than I can take. I slam down the phone.

What I do next convinces me that I'm truly addicted to Steve. I make him the reservation at the Junipine Lodge even though I'm now certain he's planning to spend New Year's Eve with HER.

I'm minding my P's and Q's, but it doesn't change the fact that more than anything I want Steve and my perfect life back.

# CHAPTER SEVENTEEN
## A NEW BEGINNING

*July, 1994*
*The office of Dr. Al Silberman*
*Tempe, Arizona*

"Come on in, Monica," Dr. Al Silberman says. The doctor, a small, dark-haired man, has only a trace of his Brooklyn accent left. "You look nice today," he tells me as he precedes me down the hall to his office.

"Thank you," I reply. When it comes to Sue's rules, I've mastered the first one. I look my absolute best. My St. Johns knit suit is fabulous, every hair on my head is in place and I'm wearing my lipstick. "Is Steve here?"

"He's waiting inside," Dr. Al replies, standing back so I can enter first. I step into the room.

I think Al intends his office to look like a comfortable living room. That's hard to do in such a small space. The wall next to the door holds an overflowing bookcase. Al's rocking chair is jammed between the end of the bookcase and his tiny wooden desk which juts out from one of the long walls. An overstuffed couch fills the other long wall, while a matching chair is squeezed in beneath the window across from me.

That's where Steve sits, in the chair as far from the door

as he can get. He looks a lot less put together than I do. He's thinner, and his skin is sallow. If he took the chair to avoid me, it doesn't work.

"Hi honey," I say in my best *nothing's wrong* voice.

I cross the room—it only takes five steps—and give him a kiss. This startles him. I straighten, the corners of my mouth lifting as my lips curl into my sweetest smile. Rules number two and three in one!

Steve looks up at me. I can feel him doing his best to radiate sincerity. "Hi, babe. Did you enjoy your trip to San Diego?"

Until yesterday, when Steve's message asking for this meeting reached me through one of my friends, I had been vacationing with Sue on Coronado Island. I really needed the break. Just now, the press of my responsibilities as the primary chair for the February 1995 Cancer Gala are crushing.

Wait. That's a lie. The only thing crushing me right now is my shame over Steve's continuing affair. When it's continuing.

Since his return from The Meadows Steve's been the ball in the ping pong game of my life. One minute he's on my side of the net, swearing he wants to stay married to me. He tells me he can't live without me. He says he doesn't know why he ever left me. The next minute, he's back on HER side of the net, no doubt telling HER he hates me.

I retreat to the comfy couch and face Dr. Al who's now sitting in his chair. He almost looks trapped between his bookcase and his tiny desk. He crosses his legs as he always does at the start of a session.

"Go ahead, Steve," he says, offering my husband a nod.

"Monica, I want to come home," Steve says. "What do I have to do to come home? I'll do anything you want."

And the door on my house goes 'round and 'round. Funny, I don't remember installing a revolving door.

It's not the first time he's said this to me, but this time I'm ready for him. I've got a list. I start at the top.

"Well sweetie, if you want to come home, you're going to have to give up your girlfriend."

Steve gives me a swift, firm nod. "No problem. She's gone," he assures me. "She's as bad for me as Heroin. She's mean and evil. I'm done with her."

This isn't news. SHE's always the Evil Queen when they've been fighting. Time for issue number two.

"I want you to go back into treatment. I can't have drugs in the house," I begin.

He interrupts me before I can finish. "No problem," he starts to say.

"And I can't have you drinking," I add.

This has been our sticking point over the past months. As before, it stops Steve cold. He stares at me for a minute, fiddling with the hem of his shirt as he thinks about my request.

"I'll give up drugs," he says, not realizing he's at last confirming what I've believed from the beginning, that he's been doing drugs. I personally believe he's been buying them from someone at that restaurant of his.

"What drugs are you doing?" Dr. Al asks, pinning Steve down with his gaze.

"Um," Steve says, blinking swiftly which indicates he's thinking. "Well, Fen-Phen to lose weight."

I glance at Dr. Al. Our gazes meet. We both believe Steve's doing more than prescription drugs.

"You know, you can't be taking anything right now," Al replies gently. "Not even prescription medicines. You have Hepatitis C. Your liver won't tolerate anything."

Steve waves away Al's concern, fidgeting nervously. "No, really it's okay for me to use the Fen-phen. Besides, a liver only costs a couple hundred thousand. My dad will buy me a new one when I need it."

We both gape at him. He can't be serious.

"Steve," I protest, "no one will give you a new liver if you're using or drinking."

He shakes his head. "No, it's really okay. I'll give up the drugs if you want, but I still want to drink," he finishes.

I remain breathless over his certainty that he can buy his way out of his health problem. "I can't have you drinking around me. It's a threat to my sobriety," I reply, not adding the remainder of that sentence: and to my safety.

There's no budging me on this issue. I'd rather have Steve home and using Heroin than alcohol. High on whiskey he's too dangerous and too violent.

Dr. Silberman shifts in his chair, drawing our attention back to him. "Steve, I thought you said you'd do anything," he reminds my husband. "Monica can't have you drinking in the house if you're with her. Can you promise her that?"

"Um," Steve replies.

"I thought you said you wanted to come home," I prod again.

"Um," Steve says again.

"Didn't you just say that your girlfriend is as bad for you as Heroin?" I say.

Oops. There I go, breaking Rule number four.

"She is. It's not about her." Steve stares at me, trying to again beam sincerity at me.

Too little, too late. I've gotten a glimpse of the resentment he's hiding behind it.

"Monica, I'm dying," he tells me, a new edge to his voice. "If I want to drink, I should be able to."

His resentment piques my own. "Steve, what are you talking about? Your whole life you've done exactly what you want to do."

Fuck me, there goes Rule number two.

Steve stares at me for a long moment then looks at Dr. Silberman. The doctor watches him calmly in return. Steve's expression shifts. He looks honestly conflicted.

Standing up, he glances between me and the doctor.

"You know, let me think about it. I'll get back to you on all this."

Then, he turns and walks out of the office.

As the door closes I look at Dr. Al. "This is so crazy. What am I supposed to do? Tell me what to do."

Dr. Al shrugs. "There's not much you can do. Monica, this is about Steve and his addiction. You just happen to be caught in the middle. Here's what you need to know. Steve will keep you on this roller coaster ride with him for as long as he can. He doesn't want to make a choice, so either you keep riding with him or you accept that he isn't interested in cleaning up and you let him go."

"Let him go!" I protest, truly heartsick at the thought. "I can't do that. He'll die if I'm not there to save him."

"That's very possible," Dr. Al replies, holding up a hand to keep me from going any further into my usual protest. "You need to listen to me this time, Monica. You need to finally hear me when I tell you Steve is incapable of cleaning up. You cannot save him. No one can."


*July, 1994*
*The office of Dr. Al Silberman*
*Tempe, Arizona*

Two weeks have passed since Steve called our first meeting at Dr. Al's office. Now here we are again. I look just as good as I did fourteen days ago. Not Steve. If anything his face is even more drawn and his eyes more sunken. I think his hair looks thinner.

The only good thing about his midlife crisis ponytail is that with his hair pulled back he can't constantly comb his fingers through it. But that leaves him nothing to do with his hands except rub his face and itch at his nose. It's something he used to do when he was using Heroin. I can't prove that he's using again, but more than anything I want to. The Detective wants to validate her suspicions.

"What have you decided?" I ask him.

He glances at Dr. Al. Dr. Al gives him a nod. Steve again looks at me. "Monica, I want a divorce."

I expect to be devastated. Instead, I breathe, filling my lungs with air. It's as if I'm a swimmer making it back to the surface only an instant before drowning.

I'm done. No more rescuing. No more lies. No more wondering how or when Steve's going to embarrass me next. It's over.

That's a relief in more than one way. I was wondering what I'd do about my new young German boyfriend if Steve actually moved home.

If letting a using Steve back into my house wasn't an option for me, neither was living alone. I was terrified and my panic attacks worsened. I had to fill the space Steve left behind so I did, with a sociopath—this diagnosis benefit of Dr. Al—half my age.

All that matters is that I'm not alone.

# CHAPTER EIGHTEEN
## SIX FEET UNDER

*February, 1999*
*Paradise Valley, Arizona*

I'm studying the new real estate brochure that describes the many features that make my Clearwater Hills home special. It's my house now on paper, but to me this will always be our house, Steve's and mine. Our clean house, the one where we were supposed to have our happily ever after.

I'm selling it. I'm a real estate agent now and have been for three years.

Passing that real estate exam was one of the proudest days of my life. It proved I had what it took to be someone other than the ex-Mrs. Steve Sarli.

I sigh and set aside the brochure. Letting go of this house is going to be so fucking hard. I'll be giving up all the hopes and expectations that it represented during the first year we lived in it. I'll be giving up on sharing a clean life with Steve just like I'm still trying to give up Steve. Despite Dr. Al's insistence that Steve isn't coming back, I still hold a tiny shard of hope that one day Steve will call me and tell me that he's coming home.

The phone rings. "Hello?" I say, half expecting a solicitor.

"Monica, it's Stacy."

I nearly drop the phone. It's Steve's wife.

Something's happened to Steve!

I catch back my panic. No, Steve's fine. I talked to him earlier today.

That is, he's fine, if I don't include how dissatisfied he is in his marriage. He should have been more careful of what he wished for, because he got it.

Suddenly, I'm morbidly curious about why SHE is calling me. I slip into professional ex-wife mode. "Stacy, what a surprise. How are you? What can I do for you?"

"Can I talk to you about something?" She sounds anxious and upset.

"Sure," I reply. "What's up?"

"It's about Steve. He doesn't want to be with me and the kids. When he comes home from work he goes straight into his office and closes and locks the door. He won't spend any time with us."

I almost laugh. Who the fuck did she think she was marrying, Ward Cleaver? Then my heart hurts for Steve's children. They're the ones who really got the shit end of this stick.

"First Stacy," I say, "you need to realize that Steve never wanted to have kids. You decided that for him." She was pregnant when they married six weeks after my divorce from Steve was final. "Steve never wanted kids because Steve wants to be the kid. That's not to say he doesn't love you and your kids. It's just who Steve is."

There's silence on the other end for a long moment, then she says, "I know he's still in love with you."

She's not the only one who knows that. In fact, except for Dr. Al everyone close to me and Steve has told me they expect him to eventually come back to me. That's why I keep holding on to that bit of hope.

Even Steve makes it easy for me to think that. Not only does he call me at least once a week just to chat, his clothes are still in our house.  From time to time, he stops by to pick up a suit he wants or some forgotten pair of shoes.  Whenever I'm feeling abandoned or lonely, I go visit his clothing, telling myself that he's not really gone, he's just on an extended business trip.

That's another thing that makes putting the house on the market so hard.  In my heart I know that if he returns to me it will be while I'm living in the house we built, the one he was so proud of and no other.

To Stacy I say, "Of course he's still in love with me.  You know why?"

"Why?"  She actually sounds curious.

"Because I'm the first wife and I'll always be first.  You're the second wife and you'll always be second.  As long as you understand what your number is in this whole situation, everything will be fine."

I start to chuckle at my twisted joke only to choke back my humor when she says, "Oh, okay.  Now I understand," as if what I've said is the most rational thing she's ever heard.

It hits me that she's really struggling with Steve.  No fucking surprise there. I know how hard it is to live with him.

"I'm sure he loves you, Stacy," I tell her gently.

"Thanks," she replies and hangs up.

It's all so strange that I stand there, staring at the phone, wondering if the conversation really happened.


*Four A.M.*
*November 12, 2001*
*Scottsdale, Arizona*

As I said I keep vampire hours, so I'm up puttering around my new house, occupying my time until sleep finally overtakes me.  Doesn't everyone clean their toilets at four in the morning?

Selling the house in Clearwater Hills means I'm no longer a married socialite from Paradise Valley. Instead, I'm a single socialite from Scottsdale. As much as I like this new patio home of mine—it's located right down the street from Steve's office; he gave me the down payment for it—it's just not the same. But then, I'm only here when I'm not living in Italy.

It's as I finish the last toilet—three bedroom, two bath—that an overwhelming sensation comes over me. Steve's getting on the plane for New York in two hours. Everything inside me screams that he must not get on that plane, that something terrible will happen if he does.

I grab my phone and dial his number.

I've been worried about Steve for almost a half a year, most of which I spent in Rome where I was keeping an apartment. After 9/11 Steve insisted I come home. I've only been back for a few weeks now and most of those I've been on bed rest, recovering from surgery. I haven't yet seen Steve since my return, although we've talked frequently on the phone.

As worried as I've been, this is the first time I'm clear that Steve's in deadly danger.

His phone rings once then goes straight to voice mail.

"Steve," I say, not minding that I'm pouring my heart to his voice mail. "I know it's probably too late to stop you, but I don't want you to go to New York. Please. Stay here. See the doctor."

Steve had been at the emergency room with chest pains a few weeks ago and the E.R. doctor directed him to see a cardiologist immediately. Steve refused.

By now I'm almost crying I'm so certain he shouldn't go. "Steve, I don't know what I'll do if I lose you. Call me when you get in," I beg. Then I add, "And I want you to know I will always love you no matter what."

He didn't return my call.

*7:00 P.M.*
*November 16, 2001*
*Messinger's Mortuary*
*Scottsdale, Arizona*

On the morning of November 13, 2001 Steve was discovered dead in his room at The Plaza Hotel in New York City. One of his business associates came looking for him when Steve, who always ran ten minutes early, never showed up for his Tuesday morning meeting and didn't answer his room phone, his cell phone or his hotel room door. When the hotel manager unlocked it they found him lying on the floor, one arm stretched out as if he'd been reaching for something as he died.

There was an autopsy because in New York when an out-of-towner dies in a hotel the NYPD wants to be sure it wasn't murder. In this case it wasn't. Although the cause listed on his death certificate is a heart attack, the coroner also confirmed that Steve was completely in Cirrhosis and his liver had failed.

I got the news at my doctor's office while waiting for an appointment and collapsed right there on the examining room floor. God bless the doctor's wife. Instead of patting me on the back and saying "There, there," like someone else might have done, Barbara Ketover took me by the shoulders, gave me a quick shake and said, "Call your lawyer right now. Get him started on your claims this minute."

I did and he has, but that doesn't make the hole in my heart feel any better.

Now I'm standing outside Steve's visitation room, waiting for the nice mortuary manager to open the casket for me. Although Stacy ordered a closed casket for the memorial service, she agreed to give me some privacy with Steve so I can say my final goodbye. I told her I needed to see him so I can have my closure, and she honored that for me.

I have to see Steve. Only when I acknowledge it's really him in that casket, that he's really dead, will I stop harboring the delusion that he isn't really gone. Or that he won't finally return to me from that extended business trip of his.

In the same conversation Stacy told me, "You'll never believe this. The New York police called a little while ago. They say Steve was with a hooker when he died. They have her on the hotel security cameras running out of his room."

No fucking surprise there, about either the hooker or that she fled the scene. I'm waiting for the final shoe to drop, convinced the police will confirm that Heroin was involved.

I anxiously watch the manager in his gentle gray suit solemnly lift the lid of Steve's mahogany casket by its ornate brass handle. As much as I need to face the truth I'm equally terrified that confronting it will leave me feeling as alone and unprotected as I did all those years in the corner of that fucking dining room.

Tears once again dribble down my face. I've been a fucking leaky faucet these past few days.

"Here baby," says Dracula, handing me a fresh tissue. "If you're going to keep crying like this I'll go get a box."

I'm the only one I know who can feel alone and unprotected in the presence of the biggest, baddest, scariest man I've come across since I left The Projects in Kansas City. He's with me tonight because I'm too messed up to drive.

My Dracula—that's what he calls himself—isn't a Transylvanian. Instead he's a big Latino with enough confidence to wear his black hair in a long ponytail and dark sunglasses inside at night. He's an artist, singer, and an attorney who once spent time in prison for murder. I met him through a real estate deal and we've since become friends. Just friends. I'm too old for him. His tastes run to eighteen-year-olds.

Why would I choose to befriend such a man? Well, first he's been a good client, but after that it's what I'm calling the Terry Kelton effect. Anyone not scarier than Terry is okay in my book. Normal men, the kind that normal women marry, don't interest me. I'm more comfortable around guys who are a little dark and dangerous.  Or maybe it's that dark and dangerous men are comfortable around me.  I think I scare the balls off normal men.

"I can't help it," I tell Dracula.  I crane my neck to look up at him.  He's built like a linebacker and is tall enough that he towers over me.  He's not a bad looking man with his square jaw and powerful shoulders, but if you weren't me and you saw him walking toward you on a dark night you might turn and walk the other way.

"It's just so fucking unnecessary.  Steve didn't have to die.  I could have saved him if he'd just stayed with me," I moan, once more kicking myself for failing at the only job Ralph ever gave me to do: to save Steve.

Dracula makes an impatient sound.  "Okay baby, if you say so," he says, patronizing me the way he always does.  "Just hurry up.  I'll get some more tissues then keep watch at the door so no one disturbs you."

The mortuary manager offers me a subdued nod as we pass each other in the doorway.  The carpeting beneath my feet is so thick that my steps make no sound.  It's just wrong that this room is so light and airy.  There should be heavy black velvet drapes, dark brooding furniture, huge brass urns full of dead bare branches and scary organ music, not pale colored walls, rows of metal folding chairs and cheery sprays of roses, lilies and carnations.

Stopping beside the casket, I close my eyes, bracing myself then turn my gaze into its depths.  And gasp.

Fuck me! Wow, he looks good!

Like I said, I haven't seen Steve since I left for Italy months ago, but two days ago Stacy showed me a picture of him taken on Halloween a few weeks past.  I was horrified.  In the photo Steve's face is bloated and colorless, his fingers are so swollen they look like sausages.

Actually, he looked like the Pillsbury Dough Boy, which I suppose is apropos.

This Steve, the dead one, is far thinner than the one

in that picture. No fucking doubt the morticians drained at least five gallons of fluid from him just to make room for the embalming shit. He also looks almost healthy, but I put that glow of life up to the pancake foundation they've put on him. They've used too much. As the stuff dried it caked his skin. Now it's flaking off in places.

Then I realize that this is my Steve and he's dead. Although his hair is combed the way he always wore it and none of his features have changed, his face looks so strange without that spark of life.

This is my Steve and it isn't. The tears start again. I swipe at them with my already damp tissue.

"At least she didn't put you in a suit and tie," I say to him, reaching inside the coffin to straighten his shirt collar. Stacy chose a white shirt with a narrow band collar and a pair of black slacks.

I suddenly realize I'm waiting for him to respond to me. That tears me in two. Steve's gone. He's really, really gone.

"Oh Steve," I cry, "I'm so sorry. I love you. I've always loved you. I know how unhappy you've been these last years. I'm so sorry it had to end this way."

My breath catches in a sob as I open my purse and take out my wedding ring, the one that Steve gave me at St. Viator's Church in Las Vegas all those years ago, not the pretentious one he replaced this with when we still lived in Clearwater Hills.

I try to lift his upper hand. Both hands rise. I look closer and see that they're tied together with some sort of plastic string.

Balancing both his hands in one of mine, I slide my ring onto his closest little finger. "Take this with you," I say to him. "I want you to wear it for all eternity."

His finger is almost too big. It takes all my effort, so much effort that he rocks in the casket with the power of my push, to get the ring over his first knuckle.

I'm crying again. All of a sudden I can't bear the way he looks with all that makeup. It hides his real face, with its map of creases, wrinkles and little scars that makes him my Steve.

"Oh my God, Steve. They used way too much of this shit on you. You would hate the way it looks. Here honey, let me just get some of it off," I tell him, hiccupping now.

Using my damp tissue I start wiping his face, working my way from his brow over his cheeks to his chin. "There, you look much better," I tell him then my gaze catches on that narrow band collar of his shirt.

All of a sudden I want to know what his autopsy scar looks like. No, I need to know. I have to see. I want to see what they did to Steve after he was dead.

Glancing at the still closed door across the room I swiftly unbutton the front of Steve shirt. The scar runs from beneath his neck down his torso and on beyond the belt of his pants. It's dark red and Steve's held together with long black stitches.

I'm not sure if I'm satisfied or horrified. I start buttoning his shirt, but as I shift his arms to one side to get to the middle button I'm again swamped by a new need to know. I finish buttoning his shirt front and stare at his shirt sleeves.

Why wait for the police to tell me when I can confirm for myself right here and now? All I need is one glimpse of his bare forearm and I'll know. Steve's tracks are as familiar to me as his face. I'll recognize anything new.

I glance at the door. It's still closed and Dracula is still on guard outside it.

My fingers fly as I open one cuff button and shove his sleeve up above his elbow. The fabric slides easily up his lifeless arm.

I stare. I can't believe he found new spots to use on his wrist. But there they are, tucked between the thick black lines of his old tracks, a couple of what looks like short cat scratches.

Fuck me, he was using.

That only makes me cry again as I roll down his sleeve and button its cuff. "Steve, why?" I demand of him. "We were clean so long."

Somehow, the confirmation that he really was using again makes it time for me to go. I lean into the casket and place a light kiss against his cheek. "I love you, Steve."

I'm halfway back to the door before I remember. Holy shit! Steve's not being buried, he's being cremated. It was in his will.

Fuck me! These mortuary guys will take off all his jewelry and give it to Stacy. No fucking way are they giving her my wedding ring.

I leap back to the side of his casket. "Sorry, honey but I just remembered they're going to cremate your ass. I need that ring back. It's mine and I'm not letting her keep it," I tell him.

He doesn't say anything, one way or another. Grabbing his hand, I tug on my ring. It doesn't budge. I yank harder, tugging his bound arms almost over the side of the casket.

Nothing.

Grunting in exertion, I lean into the casket, grab the ring with my strongest grip and pull. And pull.

I lean back away from the casket, half-lifting him with me as I go. And pull.

It won't even twist on his finger.

With a gasp of frustration I release him. Steve bounces a little as he drops back onto the cushions that line the casket bottom. I instinctively reach in and straighten him out again.

"Sorry honey," I apologize to him again, staring in disgust at the ring. It's like the fucking thing welded itself to his bone.

I glance desperately around this room, looking for some tool to help. Soap. If only I had some soap and water, maybe I could slide it off. There's nothing even faintly like that in here.

"Well it has to come off," I inform Steve.

Reaching into the casket, I pull his bound hands close to my chest. With my fist locked around the ring, I put my foot on the side of the casket and pull with all my might.

His body lifts, his chest rising higher than his head. I pull harder. His arms are out of the casket now as he slides to the side, following their lead.

"Baby, what are you doing?"

I shriek in guilty surprise, release Steve, who drops onto his side into his casket then turn toward Dracula. "My ring. I put my ring on him then I remember he's being cremated. I need my ring back."

I grab Steve's hands to show Dracula what I mean, tug on the ring one more time and it shifts. With a final pull it slides right off and back into the palm of my hand.

"Got it," I tell Dracula with a bright but watery smile.

His chuckle is as dark and dangerous as he is. "Oh my God, I can't believe you. Come on baby, it's time to go."

I agree. It's time to move on.

Turning back to Steve, I rearrange him in the casket. After a final kiss and an "I'll always love you" I leave the mortuary and step into a whole new world, a world without Steve.

# EPILOGUE
# RETURN TO
# AMITY-VILLE HORRORS

*December 15, 1997*
*Amity Therapeutic Community*
*Tucson, Arizona*

I'm driving on I-10 just outside of Tucson after returning from Kansas City and my dad's funeral earlier today. I called Bette Fleishman right after I heard about Dad's death; she and I talk every so often these days, just to touch base and check in with each other.

Bette worried about me staying with my family in Kansas City for any length of time without someone to support me. To give me an excuse to come back right away, she invited me to join her at Amity. I'll be helping out at one of their special retreats that just happened to be scheduled to start the same day as Dad's funeral.

Bette's right to be concerned about me visiting my family. I love my family, and I know they love me, but spending time with them always takes me back into the patterns of behavior I learned in childhood. It can trigger me like nothing else.

I turn off Tanque Verde Road and into Amity's dirt parking lot. I'm still grateful for every day I spent here. What Naya and Bette gave me was the insight and tools I needed for me to clean up and stay clean when I was finally ready to take that step.

It takes me a minute to find a place to park among the buses. These aren't the friendly yellow guys used for educational transport. These bad boys are painted white and have reinforced mesh on their windows. The emblem of the California Department of Corrections is pasted on their sides.

Like I said, Bette, Naya and Rod are entertaining again and I'm sure the neighbors are thrilled.

Back when Steve and I lived here this location was almost completely undeveloped. Now it's home to some of Tucson's most expensive real estate properties. That's because of the view. Off to my left are the Rincon Mountains, to my right, the Catalinas. Mesquite, Palo Verde and Ironwood trees, their leaves sparse but still green even though it's winter, rise above Prickly Pear and Cholla cactus. Pleated and tall, multi-armed Saguaros stand among them, each one looking like a man being told to stick 'em up.

It's always colder here in Tucson than it is in Phoenix. Even though I'm wearing a sweater and jeans, I cross my arms against the chill and start for the Lodge, an expansive two-story building with a stucco exterior and tile roof. Beyond the Lodge are a number of cabins, or casitas as we call them here in the Southwest. They're tiny versions of the Lodge, all covered in stucco and tiled. Very neat and tidy.

I keep expecting some kid with a clipboard to step out and confront me. When I lived here someone was always watching Amity's front door. No one got onto the property without being screened. Not today, but this is a special day.

Opening the front door of the Lodge, I slip inside. The interior also reflects Southwestern style with its Mexican tile floor, beamed ceiling and woven Navajo rugs displayed on the white plaster walls. Not that I can see much of the room just now. It's filled with a fucking sea of men, what seems to be at least a hundred of them. Most wear prison jumpsuits and bandanas on their heads.

If their jumpsuits are a sign of their status as the presently incarcerated, their head coverings identify the Hispanic men among them. I know that if any one of those bandana boys should turn to look at me I won't see eyes, only sunglasses. And tattoos.

A uniform is a uniform is a uniform.

I keep to the wall as I creep past The Pew. Anyone who's spent time at Amity has sat on this well-worn bench, waiting to receive either penance or punishment from the powers that be. I remember my time on The Pew as Purgatory.

"Oh my God, she's arrived," Naya announces from the dais at the head of the room.

I look across the expanse and see them, my former tormentors, the three people I credit for ultimately saving my life and now my friends.

Although almost twenty years have passed since my time at Amity, Naya Arbiter is still a beautiful woman, her hair yet deep brown and her eyes still as ice-blue and piercing as ever. Bette, dressed in her usual Amity uniform, black crop pants and a gray button-down shirt, stands next to Naya. Now in her mid forties, Bette's hair is going gray. It makes her look even more like she ought to be living in one of the nearby ranchettes. I wonder if she can still turn an addict into a quivering pile of jelly with a single glance the way she used to do to me.

Standing with them on the dais is Rod Mullen, Naya's husband. He's tall and good-looking in a Marlboro Man sort of way, and every bit as tough as he looks.

On the dais with them is Mark Schettinger, the man I stole thirteen dollars from when Steve and I escaped from Amity. He hasn't aged either, meaning he still looks like the Fonz from Happy Days.

"Come on, Monica," Naya calls out, smiling and waving to me. "Come on up here and introduce yourself."

The crowd parts, men in shades, men living without

women, all turning to gawk at me. I'm too busy gaping at Naya to notice them. My heart pounds. Just a fucking moment! When Bette asked me to help out this week, she never said anything about me doing public speaking.

It doesn't matter what Bette did or didn't promise. If Naya wants me to address this crowd, I will address the crowd. No one refuses Naya. Fuck, she'd probably group me—throw me into a group therapy session—if I resist. No way am I ever doing that again.

As I join the rest of the clean and sober crowd, Naya gives me a big hug then sends me down the line to hug everyone else. After everyone has exchanged the proper greeting, she pushes me forward until I'm front and center.

"Okay, now tell them about yourself. Tell them when you were here and why. And why you and Steve decided to run away. Don't leave anything out," she instructs.

I stand, my feet frozen to the floor, looking out at the bandana boys as I nervously push my hair behind my ears. I'm so scared I'm practically seeing double.

"Hello, my name is Monica Sarli," I start, only to choke on a hysterical giggle. I want to add and I'm an addict/alcoholic as if this were some A.A. meeting on Steroids. Only Amity doesn't do the Twelve Steps.

"I was at Amity from 1984 to 1985 with my husband. We were among the first couples Bette and Naya ever treated. When I arrived at Amity I'd been a Heroin addict for fifteen years, but I had also used Cocaine and Crack Cocaine, Marijuana and any prescription drugs I could get my hands on. Crack Cocaine and Heroin had been my mainstay for the year before my arrival here."

That stirs a murmur from the tough guys in front of me. People are always surprised when I tell them what and how long I used. I don't look like an addict, which just goes to show that no one knows what an addict really looks like.

"I've been clean now eleven years and like Naya says, I didn't graduate from this program. Instead, after spending a full year here, my husband and I ran away."

"And why did you run away?" Naya prompts, shooting me a quick smile.

I know what she wants. "Because you were forcing me to prepare to graduate to the halfway house," I retort. "That meant writing my senior paper," I tell the guys, "which at the time was required of everyone before we could move on. The paper had to include a list of the people at Amity I considered my role models. I made a list, but when I looked at it all I saw were lies. I didn't even like most of the people I'd named. Right then, I should have known this meant I wasn't yet clean in my life. I might not have been using drugs anymore, but back then I hadn't yet admitted that I was addicted to more than drugs."

Although a few guys nod out in the crowd mostly what I see is my own reflection in their sunglasses. I plow on, still feeling uncomfortable in this position of authority that Naya's forced me to take.

"Then I got my feelings hurt," I say.

Harboring hurt feelings and resentment can send any addict into a fall. "After that, I tallied the wrongs I thought were being done to me, looked at Steve and said: We're out of here."

Thirteen years after the fact, it's finally time to admit to my crime. "I stole bus fare from his change jar"—I make a quick, stiff gesture toward Mark Schettinger—"just enough to get us across Tucson to the airport by city bus."

"My husband and I ran to the Circle K convenience store at the corner of Harrison and Speedway," I tell the convicts, "where we hid behind the dumpsters. We were really relieved when we got on that first bus."

Even now that phrase still has terrifying meaning for me. I stifle a laugh and glance at Naya. She's smiling back at me. I can see it in her eyes. She knows very well that back then I was terrified of losing my hair to her shaver.

"I'll just warn you that you need to stay out of Naya's

way when she cleans house. Trust me, Naya can get you to reveal everything you know. That includes something as small as taking a cotton swab from someone else's supply. Her point is to remind us of this one simple truth: that all junkies lie and our lies help us keep using."

I fall silent. All of a sudden I feel like I'm babbling or, worse, trying to impress these guys. I feel like I'm wearing skin two sizes too small. I stare uncomfortably out at the men in the room.

From the back someone shouts out, "How have you stayed clean all this time?"

For an instant the question totally stumps me. What keeps me clean? The truth is I'm clean because back on August 4, 1986 I promised myself I was done using. From then on I never once looked back and I never regretted giving up drugs and alcohol. That's really all there is to it.

But, that seems too simple to share here. Who the fuck in this room is going to believe that I stay clean just because that's what I decided to do? None of these bad-asses, that's for sure.

"While I lived here I learned three simple principles. These guys," I indicate the founding members of Amity, "insisted that I couldn't fail in my new sober life if I used them. The first principle is to never lie, not even to spare someone's feelings. Lying maintains our delusions and as long as we junkies are delusional we keep using. The second one is to always run my story. That means telling people the whole truth and nothing but the truth about what I've done and how I've used. This principle is really hard for me, because I always thought of myself as a dignified Dope fiend. When I run my story I don't come out looking very dignified.

"The last principle is to help others."

The light bulb sparks over the top of my head. Oh yeah, help others. Here's something I can talk about. "I live in the Phoenix area now and since I cleaned up I've gotten involved with a number of local charities. I do a lot of good for my community."

Naya snorts. "None of that is what keeps you clean. Just be honest," she admonishes me.

The familiar knife edge in her voice instantly transports me back to 1985 and one of Naya's marathon group therapy sessions. Just like that psycho-drama with Bette, we addicts are all locked into a casita with counselors guarding the windows. I'd been the center of attention for a good hour or more. Naya, seated in her rocking chair, was trying to get me to admit how uncomfortable I was living at Amity. I was stonewalling, afraid if I told the truth the other women would only hate me more than they already did.

At last, Naya stopped rocking and aimed that piercing gaze of hers at me. "Just be honest, Monica," she snaps at me. "For once in your sorry ass life, just be fucking honest."

"Fine," I shouted back, anger tearing through me. "You want honesty? Here it is. I can't wait to get out of here so I can leave your sorry asses behind. I'm going to have a house in Phoenix with a pool that I'm going to sit beside every day. I can't wait to leave here because I'll never have to work and I'm never going to have to look at your fucking faces ever again."

Naya smiled in approval. "Now that was honest," she said.

Remembering that day dissolves my stage fright. My eyes narrow. I look out at the men listening to me.

"Okay. You want to know what keeps me clean? It's fear of the wrath of Bette and Naya. Whatever it takes, I'm never coming back here. I will never again be on my hands and knees, scrubbing grout with my toothbrush while these two women are screaming at me."

I scan the prisoners, knowing there are murderers, drug dealers and rapists in their midst, and say, "I never want to live with people like you again."

Stunned silence fills the room.

Naya smiles like a proud parent. She pats me on the back. "See, that wasn't so bad."

And the guys begin to clap.

# CONTEST INFORMATION

Because I want to be sure you read my book, I'm giving away three eBook readers as well as gift cards for Amazon.com, Barnes & Noble and iBooks. What do you have to do to enter? Nothing more than "Like" The Men Wars on Facebook.

Here's how it works: When the number of "Likes" reaches 1500, I'll select a random name to receive the Kindle. When the "Likes" reach 5000 I'll select another random name for the Nook. You're really going to have to work to get that iPad, though, because I need 10,000 Likes before I'll select a winner for that one.

Just to keep you interested along the way there'll be drawings about every 1000 "Likes" for all sorts of prizes, everything from $5.00, $10.00 and $25.00 gift cards to online book stores to signed paperback copies of Men-ipulation and even my signed photos, as well as anything else I dream up to give away.

The drawings and the winners will both be announced via Twitter and on our Facebook page, so be sure to follow me on Twitter.

Now, turn the page and read an excerpt from Book Two of the Men Wars.

**http://www.facebook.com/pages/The-Men-Wars**
**http://www.twitter.com/TheMenWars**
**http://www.TheMenWars.com**

# READ AN EXCERPT
## FROM
# THE MEN WARS
## BOOK TWO
# MEN-STURBATION

Coming 2012

# PROLOGUE
# THE FEDS TO THE RESCUE AGAIN

*6:00 A.M.*
*May 29, 2009*
*Gilbert Arizona*

I drag my eyes open with the noise. I'm in bed. I keep vampire hours. That means I went to bed about, oh, an hour ago. My eyes drift shut again.

"Open the door!" Bam, bam, bam.

I make an irritable noise. How rude. Whoever's pounding on a door somewhere in this usually sedate cul-de-sac neighborhood of mine had better quit and soon.

Bam. Bam. Bam. "Open the door!"

That's it. I sit up. I'm going to have my boyfriend tell them to stop it. Now.

I give Johnny Cider, still deep in sleep beside me, a shake. He was only Johnny Appleseed when I carted him down to the emergency room around Christmas time two years ago. I'd been out shopping when he got frisky and combined an apple and masturbation. He became Johnny Cider as the apple he'd managed to get up where the sun don't shine started fermenting. It was removed by a surgeon the next morning.

"Wake up. Who's yelling?" I ask. That's woman-speak for *You're the guy*. You go see what's happening.

He stirs, shifting uneasily away from me as he does. It's a mark of how strained our relationship has gotten since we both lost our jobs. Like so many agents, my real estate business went down the drain at the same time the stock market crash stripped me of my investments. Johnny only lost his job last month. He'd given up a fairly secure IT position with one of the local universities to take a similar job with a suburban police department, only to have them let him go on the last day of his six month probation period. The only bright spot in my life these days is that I've been living here rent free since my landlord stopped paying his mortgage.

"I don't know," Johnny grumbles, pulling the covers over his head. That's man-speak for *Fuck you, do it yourself*.

I stare down at him, disgusted. He's sleeping off another drunk. I'm so done with him. When he's not drinking he's on the computer in his loft office, keeping secrets from me.

At least that's what I think he's doing. As long as he can't hear me in the hallway he's click-click-clicking away, but when I make the slightest noise he either shuts the laptop or minimizes the screen. When I ask what he's doing, he claims he's playing one of those build-your-own-civilization games.

In the three years we've been together this is the first time he's ever hidden anything from me. But this is also the first time in our relationship that I haven't been able to buy him the things he wants, like guitars, international vacations and clothing.

Fuck me, but he and I have become my parents. We even have my parents' Friday Fight Nights, the nights Johnny gets blasted and threatens to kick me out. That was my father's role, suggesting weekly that he was leaving my mother and us kids. Right now, I'm struggling not to play my mother's role of helpless victim—not an easy task when circumstances have left me all but a helpless victim.

"Open the door!"

I hear it again. It sounds closer now that I'm sitting up.

Bam!

Bam!

Bam!

I have to see what's happening. Slipping from our bed, I grab my little blue bathrobe and stumble down the stairs, feeling sad. I'll miss this house when I move next week. It's spacious and airy, with four bedrooms and a den that opens up into our walled front courtyard; I use that room as my office. Originally a model home, it has all the bells and whistles, including expensive wool carpeting, a pool and spa, upgraded appliances and a three car garage. The tall walls and vaulted ceilings make the perfect showcase for my art collection.

Downstairs, I round the corner and start for the door, only to freeze in astonishment. There, framed in the door's etched glass window, is a policeman in full battle mode: helmet, protective face gear, bulletproof vest. He's holding up his drawn gun. There are at least five more policemen behind him all dressed the same way, all of them showing arms.

Fuck me! Although I've been working with my landlord's lender about my move-out date, I was still getting notices saying I'd be evicted on May twenty-sixth. After the twenty-sixth passed without me getting the boot, I assumed everything was kosher.

But really, they need a fucking SWAT team to do it?

The officer sees me through the window. "Open the door, ma'am," he commands.

What the fuck choice do I have? I open the door. "Can I help you?" I ask.

Rather than answer me, he lifts me by my upper arms, swivels and half-carries me toward the sidewalk. "Who's in the house with you? Any weapons? Any animals?"

His questions pepper me like buckshot.

I give my answers as swiftly as I can. "My boyfriend.

Yes, a lot." Johnny keeps an arsenal. "No pets."

Only after I've given my answers do I consider I shouldn't have. Isn't that part of my rights, not to answer questions without a lawyer present? Do I have any rights in an eviction?

He sets me down on the sidewalk, pivots and races back for the house, shouting out my answers to the rest of the SWAT team. I watch, stunned, as they charge in through my front door.

Out here it's already warm even though it's only May. It's about to get hotter still as the sun rises to a joyous chorus of birdsong. Not that I notice. I'm looking at the yellow tape that prevents anyone from driving onto my street and the plainclothes detectives appearing out from behind each of the nine other houses that line this golf club-shaped cul-de-sac. Dawn's light, a pleasant rose and gold reaching up into a robin's egg blue sky, stains the massive police command post vehicle parked in the toe of the golf club.

What the fuck? This looks like the biggest Mafia drug bust I've ever seen. Jesus, I've got to be hallucinating. Yeah, that's what's happening. I'm still in bed and this is one really fucked up dream.

I stare at the big trailer. The light grows steadily stronger. There's no mistaking this bad boy for what it is. It might resemble a motor home in shape, but no Snowbird ever drove one with a rooftop covered with that many antennae.

The door of the vehicle opens and a female officer exits. Latina and attractive, her dark hair casually styled, she crosses the street to stand beside me. Her badge hangs by a cord around her neck, just like in CSI. Her polo shirt is plain and mannish, her pants, khaki and she wears those funky black police boots.

I'm more of a Manolo Blahnik girl myself.

"Is this about the foreclosure?" I ask.

She gives me a puzzled look. "I don't think so."

She doesn't know? What the fuck is this? And, if this

isn't about the foreclosure then something's really wrong here. "I think you might have the wrong house. Can you tell me what's going on?"

"No, they'll explain it to you later," she replies cryptically and that's it, the sum total of our conversation.

Together, me in my bathrobe and her in her casual uniform, we stand on the sidewalk in the uncomfortable heat of this May morning, watching as officers, both uniformed and plainclothes, armed or not, begin streaming in and out of my house. Some carry cameras, others have boxes.

After about ten minutes, Johnny appears in the doorway, an officer at his side. They stop in the courtyard. Johnny doesn't look at me and we're not close enough to speak. Two detectives, moving with an air that suggests they're in charge, then take him back inside the house.

After that, my detective-escort leads me inside and sits me in my family room where I'm commanded to "Stay."

The minutes tick by. At the end of an hour all I know is that this team is led by the Phoenix police department. That's makes me even more certain this is a colossal mistake. I mean, what the fuck does Phoenix PD care about a foreclosure in Gilbert, some thirty miles off their home turf? Someone's made a typo.

As I start into my second hour of watching the police move through my home, I'm beginning to add up one and one and come up with fifteen. Is this raid because of my relationship with Dracula, my bad-ass Latino attorney friend with his fingers in a lot of strange pies?

I discard that idea. Dracula might be a bad-ass, but he's a very careful one.

Can this have something to do with Terry Kelton, my former psychopathic best friend and drug kingpin of Kansas City? Not possible. With my help and Terry's approval the Feds put Terry away for life in prison.

Then what the fuck is this?

At the hour and a half mark a couple of grinning detectives come into the family room. They look very casual in jeans, polo shirts and their trainers. Even with their hair trimmed military-short the only thing that distinguishes them as police officers are the badges hanging around their necks.

"Those are some closets you've got up there," one of them says to me, a lift of his hand indicating the two smaller of the upstairs bedrooms. I'm using those bedrooms to store my clothes and shoes. "I can't believe you've got everything color-coded and organized. Are you running a store or something? You must have at least six hundred pairs of shoes."

Despite the strangeness of this day, I can't help but smile. "No store. And it's closer to a thousand pair. They're all mine. What can I say? I'm a clothing and shoe whore." An expensive clothing and shoe whore. Like I said, I'm a Manolo Blahnik girl. "So why are you here today? Is this about the foreclosure? Can I make a phone call?"

His expression shutters like a curtain being drawn. "Sorry ma'am, not now." He and his partner move swiftly away.

Gee-zuz!

At the two hour mark the two detectives I've pegged as the leaders of this weird excursion appear in my family room. "I'm Detective Curly," one of them says, introducing himself. He's a big guy and I can tell he works out. In his forties, he has sandy hair and pale eyes. He looks totally hot in his navy polo shirt stenciled with the words Phoenix PD. "Why don't you join my partner and me for a conversation?"

Still in my robe, I follow them out to that command post. It's really interesting inside, like a very narrow police station on wheels. Everything is scaled down to fit. One man sits at a tiny desk that juts from the wall, typing into a laptop. Another officer sits in an equally as small chair, speaking on a cell phone. He's using all those buzz words I've heard on every TV cop show I've watched.

Once I enter the tiny private office at the back of the

trailer with Detective Curly and his partner, the door is shut. Detective Curly indicates that I should take the chair across from his. It's small enough that I feel like I'm in kindergarten again. I wonder how comfortable its twin is for a man as big as him. There's no desk between us and no other chair, so his partner leans back against the wall, his arms crossed over his chest. His attitude suggests he's there more to listen than speak.

Facing me, Detective Curly begins with, "Can you please state your name?"

I gape at him. "Monica Sarli. You don't even know who I am? What is this about? I really think you've got the wrong house here."

"No ma'am, we're in the right place," he assures me. "Before we get started, I need to read you your rights."

I rear back into my chair, shocked and suddenly feeling trapped. Fuck me! I haven't done anything illegal since my Terry Kelton days. "For what? Am I being arrested? Do I need to call a lawyer?"

I'm steadied by my own words. I do have rights. I'm not trapped. My eyes narrow.

I point a finger at him. "Look, you need to tell me what this is about. Only then will I know if I'm going to talk to you or not."

He stares at me for moment, his gaze guarded as if he's considering my demand. He relents with a blink. "This is not about you."

There is such conviction and assurance in his voice that I settle more easily into my chair. He's just made me a promise. I'm not going anywhere today I don't want to go. Thank God. Prison just doesn't work for me. I wouldn't like the food or the clothes, especially not the shoes.

I let him read me my rights. I feel like I've been sucked into one of any of the cop shows I've ever watched. This seems so surreal.

When he's done, he leans back a little in his small chair,

crosses his arms and says, "Ma'am, my partner and I head up sting operations for the Phoenix Task force on child pornography."

That knocks the air out of my lungs. Of all the things I expected to hear this is not one of them. Every fiber of my being rejects any possibility of some connection between me or Johnny and kiddie porn.

"What?! Now, I'm sure you've got the wrong house."

His gaze softens and he gives a shake of his head. "Oh no, ma'am. We are definitely at the right house. So tell me, is Johnny Cider your boyfriend and how long have you been together?"

A year ago I would have proudly said yes then looked at Johnny with love in my eyes. Then again, a year ago I was still flush with cash and thinking that he and I would spend the rest of our lives together. We talked about it often. We don't anymore. So is he my boyfriend?

"For the moment," I hedge. "We met in '06 and moved in together in '07."

Detective Curly nods as if the movement of his head causes his brain to record my response. I've seen that movement before, back when the FBI was interviewing me and my ex-husband about Terry Kelton. Maybe it's a memory technique they teach in law enforcement school.

"We've been monitoring your computers since June of '08," the detective tells me now. "We got the heads up that someone was looking at stuff he shouldn't be from your IP address. I notice the two of you are on some swinger sites."

"That's not against the law," I point out, still struggling to absorb what he's saying. They've been monitoring my computer? What's an IP address? Computers and I have a real love-hate relationship.

"No, it's not," he agrees, then takes a few papers off a shelf behind him and hands them to me. "Here, read this. The person writing this thinks he's corresponding with a thirteen-year-old girl. Tell me if it sounds like Johnny."

The printout is just text. No, it's not just anything; it's dirty sex talk. I instantly recognize the sexual suggestions and comments as the ones Johnny has said to me while we're fucking. It's word for word, the same adjectives, the same sentence structure. There's no mistaking the way Johnny expresses himself. His grammar, like his accent, is very London posh.

I'm floored. The police didn't make this up. Johnny really wrote this.

It's not like I didn't know Johnny had some strange fetishes. I'd put that up to his upbringing. Not only is he the product of the upper crust British Public School system, a system infamous for sexual abuse, he was molested by a family member.

But I'm absolutely certain he's no pedophile. I'm also a victim of childhood molestation, and I would know if he were.

Not that it matters now. When he wrote this he completely crossed the line with me. No man in my life is going to fantasize about a child. We're done and he's gone.

That's when the lightning bolt hits. Oh. My. God. The SWAT team is here to save me!

With that, I throw Johnny under the bus and never look back, telling the nice detective everything I know, including how I think Johnny's been stealing my prescribed Testosterone (hey, women of a certain age need a boost) and that he's had to use the little blue pill more than once lately. I mention Johnny's increased drinking, the verbal abuse he showers on me when he's drunk and how different this is from when I first met him. I also tell him how Johnny has started minimizing the screen or closing the laptop cover when he thinks I'm coming into his office.

The detective isn't taking notes. I'm guessing this means I'm not telling him anything he doesn't already know. Maybe all he wants from me is validation or to discern if I'm involved.

When I'm done, Detective Curly smiles at me and leans back in his tiny chair. It creaks as if the nails might pop. "I appreciate your cooperation. Now, I understand that you've been asking about the foreclosure. Did you really think someone would bring a SWAT team to do an eviction?"

I laugh, totally enjoying the joke with my new best friend. "Well, it did seem a little bit dramatic."

That's my life, one drama after another. Welcome to Men-sturbation, Book Two of The Men Wars. It's as whacked out as Book One but instead of drugs there's Interpol, gorgeous Italian men and even more gorgeous Italian shoes, the Riviera, and sex. Lots of sex.

And the saga continues. . .

# A NOTE FROM DENISE DOMNING:

First, I need to say a few thank yous. To Monica, who knew we'd become such good friends, but I'm so glad we did. Sorry for the dirt on my shoes and under my nails. Thank you, Ed, for living through this project with me. Real live characters are a whole lot different than the kind I usually keep in my head. Also, to Amber Anderson, for being my back up and having InDesign when I needed it.

Special thanks go to Katie Kotchman, our agent, for believing in us from the first nineteen pages I sent via Denise Marcil. And Denise, I'm so glad I knocked you off your chair all those years ago.

As you can imagine, after writing eleven historical romances, the last thing I thought I'd be doing was co-writing someone's memoir, especially someone whose path would never have crossed mine except for the writing project. So how did Monica and I connect?

Through Barbara Ketover, the wife of Dr. Alan Ketover, our shared MD/Homeopath. At almost every visit Barbara, who knew very well I wrote fiction, would insist I had to meet this woman and write her book. She finally wore me down and the rest, as they say, is history. Thank heavens it only took me five years to research Monica's life as compared to the twelve years I spent studying the Twelfth Century before completing my first novel.

And I did do my research. I walked Kansas City with Monica, spoke to her family and friends, read all her letters (Monica saves everything, luckily for me) and perused thousands of pictures. Once I was sure all her stories were true, I was ready to write, or rather channel, because that's what I've been doing. I sit next to Monica typing furiously as she talks. After that, I make real sentences, remove half the fucks (Monica is the only one I know who uses that word as noun, verb, adjective and adverb) and clean up the grammar. Her stories are all hers and I've had quite the ride putting them on paper.

I hope you've enjoyed them as much as I have.

Denise Domning
Denise@themenwars.com
www.denisedomning.com

Printed in Great Britain
by Amazon

30321304R00129